EDITORIAL

Too many secrets

In 1988, at the height of Thatcherism, and again in 1995, *Index* reported on the state of liberty in Britain. For citizens of a democratic society, these files did not make particularly cheerful reading. Then, in 1996, Tony Blair made a grand and categorical pledge to introduce freedom of information – 'a change that is absolutely fundamental to how we see politics developing in this country' – if Labour came to power. Now, as Nick Cohen so eloquently reveals, we seem once again to be seeing a government seduced by the pleasures of power and control; any freedom of information legislation is in danger of being seriously compromised.

Would that Britain's often slavish imitation of America (where freedom of information has been in place for more than three decades) were in evidence here, but no such luck. 'We cannot,' says Jack Straw, now the steward of the bill, 'be led all the time by international examples.' Americans, of course, remain amazed at our tolerance of this culture of secrecy, at what we are not allowed to publish, at what they see as our complacency in defending our liberties.

Disturbingly, the new institutions of Europe are similarly obsessed with obfuscation and secrecy. The six blank pages in this issue draw attention to how the European Commission will protect its officials rather than acknowledge the findings of its own investigators. *Index*, to protect the journalist concerned, has not been able to publish this story. But only the media, it seems, can hold this Leviathan to account, and it is not proving easy, as Martin Walker makes clear.

Our file on Ireland is written in the wake of two terrible tragedies, Ballymoney and Omagh. The Peace Agreement has not, yet, brought peace. But the people of Ireland, north and south, have spoken, have voted Yes. The murders were committed by a minority who voted No. Our contributors, north and south, write on the assumption that no person nor group can subvert the people's decision.

Two great poets, one Polish, one Czech, died in July. Zbigniew Herbert and Miroslav Holub represented what Al Alvarez calls 'the survival of ordinary human values – sanity, decency, self respect – in an ocean of corruption and hypocrisy'. Their authority as poets was also a moral authority, not a role writers in the West are accustomed to. *Index* salutes them. ❑

contents

EuroMedia: a continent retreats from truth

p32

Ireland: Bordering on peace

p126

INDEX

INDEX ON CENSORSHIP 5 1998

WEBSITE NEWS UPDATED EVERY TWO WEEKS

INDEX
ON CENSORSHIP

www.indexoncensorship.org
contact@indexoncensorship.org
tel: 0171-278 2313
fax: 0171-278 1878

Volume 27 No 5 September/November 1998 Issue 183

Index on Censorship (ISSN 0306-4220) is published bi-monthly by a non-profit-making company: Writers & Scholars International Ltd, Lancaster House, 33 Islington High Street, London N1 9LH. *Index on Censorship* is associated with Writers & Scholars Educational Trust, registered charity number 325003 *Periodicals postage*: (US subscribers only) paid at Newark, New Jersey. Postmaster: send US address changes to *Index on Censorship* c/o Mercury Airfreight International Ltd Inc, 365 Blair Road, Avenel, NJ 07001, USA
© This selection Writers & Scholars International Ltd, London 1998
© Contributors to this issue, except where otherwise indicated

Subscriptions (6 issues per annum)
Individuals: UK £39, US $52, rest of world £45
Institutions: UK £44, US $80, rest of world £50
Speak to Syra Morley on 0171 278 2313

5   EDITORIAL Ursula Owen Too many secrets

8   OBITUARIES Miroslav Holub and Zbigniew Herbert

10   IN THE NEWS

        NEWS ANALYSIS
16   IRAN Nilou Mobasser By any other name
18   IRAN Mohammad Reza Za'eri When in doubt
21   NIGERIA Christine Anyanwu Rats on two legs

        NEWS FEATURE
26   MIDDLE EAST Jo Glanville Lines of attack

32   COVER STORY: EUROMEDIA
34   Martin Walker Brussels spouts
40   The white pages EC Corruption
46   Duncan Campbell Listening in silence
55   Nick Cohen Go for the full monty, Tony!
61   Robert Cockcroft A world of your own
64   Julian Petley An unsavoury business
69   Paul O'Connor 'You have the right to remain silent...'

72   OPINION Tatyana Tolstoya Colors of confusion

78   INDEX INDEX

        LITERATURE
108   BURMA Nita Yin Yin May Under the dragon
111   BURMA Rory MacClean Love in a hot climate
117   JAMES JOYCE Judith Vidal-Hall Ulysses' journey
122   RADCLYFFE HALL Sarah A Smith Breaking the code

126   IRISH FILE
127   Michael Foley & John O'Farrell Bordering on peace
130   Seamus Heaney The Glamoured
133   John O'Farrell Murdering the future
141   Luke Gibbons Radical memory
144   Robert Fisk & Frankie Quinn Borders
156   Dominic Bryan & Neil Jarman Parades and power
161   Michael Foley A people's press
165   Richard Kearney Beyond sovereignty
170   Michael Foley One law for all
173   Mairtin Crawford On the streets of Belfast

176   BABEL Iran Wear the chador on the inside
182   CINEMA Edward Lucie-Smith Letter from Pärnu
188   NEW MEDIA Russell Baird Tewksbury Cache 22

Miroslav Holub 1923 – 1998

Miroslav Holub, who died on 14 July, was in many respects a Renaissance man: a scientist, an immunologist and a writer who was not so much a Czech poet as an international poet who happened to write in Czech. Many of his poems deal with truth as something that cannot be manipulated or commanded by those in power, and it is easy to see why the communist regime, which silenced him for so long, regarded him with suspicion or even downright hostility. The persecution to which he was subjected was the kind of surrealist harassment that he might himself have though up in his poetry and which, indeed, he described in 'Angels of Extermination, Angels of Exclusion' (*Index*, 5/97). His sudden death has deprived the world of a major writer who was still at the peak of his creative powers. **Ewald Osers**

Casualty

They bring us crushed fingers,
mend it, doctor.
They bring us burnt-out eyes,
hounded owls of hearts,
they bring us a hundred white bodies,
a hundred red bodies,
a hundred black bodies,
mend it, doctor.
On the dishes of ambulances they bring
the madness of blood,
the scream of flesh,
the silence of charring,
mend it, doctor.

And while we are suturing
inch after inch,
night after night,
nerve to nerve,
muscle to muscle,
eyes to sight,
they bring in
even longer daggers,
even more thunderous bombs,
even more glorious victories,

idiots.

Translated by Ewald Osers

Zbigniew Herbert 1924 - 1998

Zbigniew Herbert, who died on 28 July, was born in Lwow in Poland and lived through the successive German and Russian occupations of his homeland. His poetry was first published in 1956, when the communist regime allowed a brief thaw in their repression of dissenting artists and writers. During this period, Herbert was able to travel in western Europe and, in London became aquainted with a community of expatriates who began to translate his work into English. Herbert's poetry speaks of individuals at the mercy of overwhelming power. But this is no remorseless litany of suffering; rather, his poems delight in the small, ordinary and familiar, portraying the triumph of 'the little people' against the forces of darkness he knew so well, with humour and compassion. The humanity he celebrated is the poorer for the loss of one of the great poets of our century. *EM*

Pebble

The pebble
is a perfect creature

equal to itself
mindful of its limits

filled exactly
with a pebbly meaning

with a scent which does not remind one of anything
does not frighten anything away does not arouse desire

its ardour and coldness
are just and full of dignity

I feel a heavy remorse
when I hold it in my hand
and its noble body
is permeated by false warmth

       – Pebbles cannot be tamed
       to the end they will look at us
       with a calm and very clear eye

Translated by Czeslaw Milosz

● **Viagra: The Movie** The libido-phobic British Board of Film Classification, responsible for screening the UK's intake of film and video, has hit upon an intriguing form of deconstructivism to liberate itself in preparation for the next century. Speaking on the publication of its annual report, director James Ferman queried: 'Next month we have Viagra coming. Why should it be that we are allowed to be chemically aroused but not visually?' He urged a relaxation of the UK's pornography laws in the light of the growing number of people leading solitary, 'vicarious' sex lives.

● **Vitamins: a truth-free zone** Americans were given until 27 August to petition members of Congress about proposals by the Food & Drug Administration that will make it illegal to inform 'customers' how vitamins affect certain illnesses. Phrases, such as 'reduces nausea associated with chemotherapy', 'protects against cancer' and 'treats hot flashes', will be classified as 'illegal speech'.

● **That's that, then?** Anglican bishops declared on 5 August that homosexual relations are 'incompatible with scripture', opposed the ordination of practising homosexuals and affirmed traditional teachings that sex is permissible only within marriage. After a divisive debate among church leaders attending the once-in-a-decade Lambeth conference, a compromise resolution was toughened by conservative African bishops, who said homosexuality was against biblical law. The final resolution was backed by 526 bishops and opposed by 70, with 45 abstentions.

● **Three strokes and you're out** Men winking at Tanzanian women face the prospect of a lengthy jail term under a Special Offences Provisions bill passed in June, that defines the repetitive, ocular gesture as sexual harrassment falling barely short of outright rape. The bill, passed under pressure from a public enraged by sexual assaults on women, allows for a five-year term for men caught winking thrice. It is not yet clear whether the object of the gesture must be the same in each incident.

● **Papal bull** *Philadelphia Inquirer* reporter Ralph Cipriano is suing his editor, a move so unusual that no-one can recall a precedent. Cipriano is seeking US$50,000 plus punitive damages from Knight-Ridder, the newspaper's owner, and *Inquirer* editor Robert Rosenthal for what the suit calls 'false and defamatory statements,' 'innuendo' and 'malicious libel'. The dispute stems from Cipriano's decision to investigate the local Catholic archdiocese for the *National Catholic Reporter*. He indicated in June that he'd had trouble getting the *Inquirer* to publish allegations of mismanagement by Cardinal Anthony Bevilaqua who, he said, 'was a sacred cow at my newspaper'. Rosenthal said 'there were things we didn't publish that Ralph wrote that we didn't think were truthful.'

● **Mint-imperfect** The new Bosnian mark, introduced by the OECD as the Balkans' only convertible currency, has run into a spot of bother over orthography. The 10-mark note used in the Bosnian Serb republic bears the name of the poet Aleksa Santic in Roman script, rather than Cyrillic, while the five-mark note also has the denomination in Roman. The one-mark bill is spot-on in Cyrillic, but the writer Ivo Andric – a past-master at describing Bosnia's ethnic fissures – is spelled with the phonetic letter 'dj', instead of 'c', an unforgivable aspersion on the Nobel winner's origins. The Central Bank governor said the mistakes were due to 'haste ... and inadequate proof-reading' and would have to be reprinted. The currency was, nevertheless, launched on 22 June – although the provocative one-mark note was not circulated in the Bosnian Serb republic.

● **Piggy in the window**
Author of *Trainspotting* Irvine
Welsh has attracted the attention of
Hampshire Constabulary. Posters
advertising his latest novel, *Filth*,
were taken down from the
windows of a Southampton book
shop, October Books, on police
orders. It seems the local bobbies
found the central image of a pig's
head wearing a police helmet
'distressing', and a little-known
clause in the Criminal Justice Act
prohibits any public display that
might cause the boys in blue such
emotional upset. Imagine their
horror then, after the daring raid
on tiny October Books, to find
that the windows of all the town's
larger bookstores were suddenly
displaying *Filth*. The confiscated
posters have now been returned.
FF

● **Gay raiders** The new
Blairite Puritans have a long reach.
On 18 May, five customs cars and
a police car rolled up to the rural
Norfolk headquarters of the UK's
oldest established homosexual
publishers, Gay Men's Press, and
searched the premises from top to
bottom. They also confiscated all
their computers and discs.

What were they after? The
press had been sent – unsolicited
from abroad – a German-language
academic book on paedophilia.
Labour's famous 'out-as-gay' MPs
fled from the scene when asked for

help, and it was left to Tony Benn
to take up the parliamentary
cudgels. Dawn Primarola, minister
in charge of customs, replied to
Benn's query by saying loftily that
the action was entirely justified
'because these paedophiles often
claim things are sent unsolicited'.

A month later, thanks to the
efforts of a persistent solicitor, the
material was returned. No
prosecution has been mounted.
Aubrey Walker, director of GMP,
says, 'We were completely taken
aback because nothing like this had
ever happened to us in our 20
years of publishing.' No: not even
under Mrs Thatcher.

Why has the story stayed under
wraps until now? Because GMP,
probably rightly, were afraid of
retaliation from the locals. **ELS**

Credit: Twelve Stars

● **and once as farce** Clear
parallels with Nazi propaganda are
evident in a Web-based cartoon
espousing European Monetary
Union. 'Captain Euro' is the work
of Twelve Stars Communications

and is promoted as repackaging the 'great product' that is Europe and alleviating Europe's 'identity crisis'.

Captain Euro is a turbo-charged EU Ombudsman who leads the 'goodies' against evil Dr D Vider and his global conspiracy. Euro's campaign is kickstarted by the discovery of wondrous artifacts in an ancient Viking longship – his Aryan roots are thus established. Dr David Vider on the other hand, is an unethical multi-millionaire and currency speculator. In appearance, he is besuited, small and sharp, with a pointed goatee and a hooked nose. His company Dividex is a rootless operation that wanders the world under the auspices of the Global Touring Circus, recruiting 'baddies' and covertly running hundreds of businesses across Europe.

Nicholas De Santis of Twelve Stars claims his company was not aware that depicting the friends and enemies of Europe in this way was resonant of Goebbels' characterisation of Aryans and non-Aryans in the 1930's. Specifically, he didn't find anything sinister in the impressive parallels between his creation, 'Dr D Vider', and Goebbels' grotesque Jewish bankers supposedly acting to impoverish Germany. He warns against 'taking this too seriously'. 'It's about entertainment, not about politics'.

It is, however, about politics.

The characters are to be used to promote the European Union and EMU in schools and to represent Europe worldwide. Twelve Stars' clients include the European Parliament and the European Movement, Britain's pro-EU campaigning group. The worry is not that Twelve Stars is seeking to ressurect Nazism, because the company clearly isn't. What is disturbing is that people so closely involved with crafting Europe's future, are so blissfully ignorant of Europe's past. *Elizabeth Prest*

● **Feeling the squeeze** The Asian economic crisis is sparing no-one. Daily-wage earners and financial executives are both complaining. Even journalists are feeling the pinch as their industry is being forced to retrench throughout the region.

In Thailand, journalists have turned to the sex industry to survive. According to the Reporters Association of Thailand, some 4,500 media workers – 1,500 journalists among them – have lost their jobs since the Thai *baht* was floated in July 1997. The number of daily and weekly newspapers has dropped from more than 20 to 10. 'Some Thai journalists, especially women, are now working as hostesses in clubs,' said Kavi Chongkijthavorn, editor of Thailand's *The Nation*. 'Because of the economic crisis, more people have entered the flesh trade.'

Many journalists are demoralised, Chongkijthavorn said, forced to work as freelance writers or offer their services to politicians and public relations groups. This new breed of journalists, known as 'the spin doctors', packages issues, politicians and businessmen like commodities for sale. Supinya Klangnaron, a Thai mass communications graduate who now works as a non-government volunteer, said the crisis had seen a change in journalists' lifestyle. 'They don't go out that much anymore and they are selling things to survive: mobile phones, computers, even mementos like reporters' notebooks autographed by news sources or taped interviews.' Why people are buying the stuff, she reflected, was another matter.

'Newspapers are discovering that the economic downturn they have been reporting on for nearly a year is not sparing them,' said Sonny Inbaraj, a former *Bangkok Post* staffer who now runs *The AustralAsian*, an online newspaper based in Darwin. 'They are being forced to fire staff and cut operations at a time when their reader's need for information is more crucial then ever,' he added. Even prestigious newspapers, like *The Nation* and the *Bangkok Post* have had to lay off staff.

Elsewhere in Asia, the situation is little different. Despite the new-found openness that has followed the collapse of the Suharto regime, Indonesia's 300 or so newspapers and magazines find themselves in a bind. With the collapse in the local currency, newsprint costs up by 100 per cent and advertising revenue cut by half and expected to fall by another 30 per cent this year, many, like the leading Bahasa Indonesia daily *Kompas*, are subsidising printing costs in order to survive.

In the Philippines, newspaper prices have risen to offset the 50 per cent fall in advertising revenues; industry analysts in Malaysia expect newsprint costs, which account for some 40 per cent of total costs, to rise by 50 per cent next year. **José Torres Jr**

● **Clash of language** The hasty enactment of a new language law, hard on the heels of the assassination of a popular Berber singer, has crystallised a long-simmering clash between Algeria's two rival cultures, the majority Arabic and the Berber.

On 5 July, only two weeks after the assassination of the popular Berber singer, Lounes Matoub, allegedly by an squad of militant GIA insurgents, the government decreed the long-delayed implementation of a law making Arabic the sole official language.

Many see in its timing a sop to militant Islamists who have long advocated an Arab-Islamic identity cleansed of all 'foreign' influences.

Berber fury exploded at a succession of rallies where both the government and Islamists came under fire. The new law requires all government offices, educational institutions and political parties to conduct their business in Arabic. It will, for example, be a punishable offence for any politician in the Berber-dominated Kabilya region to address a crowd in Tamazight, the most widely used of the 14 Berber dialects spoken in Algeria. The 5 million Berbers in Algeria's 30 million population, have persistently resisted attempts by authoritarian governments to impose an Arab-Islamic identity on a culture that predates the arrival of Islam in Algeria by centuries.

In 1963, a cultural movement was founded to demand state recognition for Berber language and culture. It reached its apogee with a 1980 rising of Kabylie students after the government banned a prominent professor of literature from lecturing on the history of Berber poetry. By the early 1980s, the cultural battle lines were clearly drawn between the rising force of Islamic activists and the more secular-minded Berber language activists. Lounes Matoub's songs conveyed the

double sense of betrayal felt by the Berbers towards francophones and Islamists, both of whom aimed to extinguish cultural pluralism.

Following the introduction of political pluralism in 1989, Berber political and cultural activists came together to launch the Rally for Culture and Democracy (RCD). The RCD rules out any deal with the Islamists and holds fast to its twin pillars of secularism and anti-Islamism. A second Berber-dominated party, the Socialist Forces Front (FFS), led by Hocine ait Ahmed, favours dialogue with the Islamists but is committed to defying the arabisation law.

The recent formation of an Armed Berber Movement (AMB), which seeks to avenge the death of the musician Lounes Matoub and fight the government's language drive, is a disturbing indication of the direction things could take if the government persists with a divisive and untimely policy.
Arif Azad

Index 4/98: Correction

We wish to apologise for an unfortunate error in which Günter Grass was described as a 'winner of the Nobel Prize for Literature'. Strangely, this is not the case and we apologise for any confusion this may have caused. ❏

NILOU MOBASSER

By any other name

Phoenix-like, Iran's most popular paper rose each morning from the ashes of censorship with new plumage

Iranian politicians today can be roughly divided into two groups. Those who are popular and have little power, and those who are unpopular but control almost all the instruments of power. The two groups are virtually at war if for no other reason than that, by the very nature of things, it is hard to see how they can coexist indefinitely. In the meantime, the Iranian nation watches this game of ping-pong or cat and mouse, and acts with astounding maturity, courage and determination whenever the occasion demands or allows it.

From the moment Iranians went en masse to the polling stations on 23 May 1997 and, as if by a secret, prior arrangement, cast their votes for the candidate who was not meant to win – electing Mohammad Khatami as president – they have refused to 'go away'. Whether it is by voting when they think it might do some good, or by refusing to vote when the choice is absurdly limited – as they did in parliamentary by-elections in March 1998 – they insist on making their wishes known in the most constructive, effective and unmistakable way, as if they were all graduates in political science.

Reflecting the mood of the nation, Iranian newspapers have never been so interesting. And the people can again make their wishes known by spending their hard-earned rials on the papers of their choice. Two relative newcomers to the press world, both established after Khatami's election victory, were *Jameah* (pro-Khatami) and *Farda* (anti-Khatami).

By July, *Farda* had gone bankrupt, while *Jameah*'s circulation had reached a respectable 300,000, a figure not so much limited by demand but by problems with printing facilities and paper supplies (*Index* 4th/98).

In some quarters, *Jameah*'s popularity was probably seen as its greatest crime; in what was undoubtedly an orchestrated move to shut it down, a series of complaints was lodged against it by a number of like-minded plaintiffs. The case was heard by the press jury which found *Jameah* guilty on some counts and not guilty on others, recommending leniency in sentencing in view of the fact that this was the first time the paper had been taken to court. (The managing directors of Iranian newspapers spend an impressive amount of time in court.) The judiciary ruled to revoke the newspaper's licence, the harshest sentence it could have handed down. Not surprisingly, *Jameah* appealed against the ruling.

On Thursday 23 July, the same day Gholamhoseyn Karbaschi, mayor of Tehran and one of Iran's most popular and intelligent officials, was sentenced to five years in prison, the appeal court upheld the verdict against *Jameah*. The judiciary's (unpopular) senior officials must have felt well pleased with themselves by the end of that day.

On Saturday 25 July, a new national daily, *Tous,* hit the news stands. A prominent masthead declared: '*Tous* at the service of society' (the word for society being – *Jameah*). And it wasn't difficult to see that *Tous* was, indeed, *Jameah* by any other name. The entire staff of the banned paper, including the indomitable editor-in-chief, Mashallah Shamsolvaezin, had taken over *Tous,* formerly a provincial paper that had itself run foul of the authorities in 1995.

Needless to say, the judiciary was not amused. After a few statements to the effect that the relevant (popular) minister should put an end to this 'ploy' and a few statements by the minister saying there was no law preventing the staff of one paper going to work for another, on 31 July, the head of the judiciary, Ayatollah Mohammad Yazdi, delivered the Friday sermon in Tehran and made his displeasure abundantly clear. 'The people,' he said, 'would not tolerate such deceit.' The minister had better halt the publication of *Tous,* or else.

As if in response to Yazdi's sermons, an angry group of about 20 to 30 people gathered outside the *Tous* office the next day, chanting slogans against the paper and its staff. Shamsolvaezin himself was punched in the face by one of the demonstrators. A few hours later, the judiciary banned *Tous.* The minister appealed for the ban to be lifted.

On Sunday 2 August, yet another new daily appeared on the news-stands published by the same company that had published *Jameah* and *Tous.* Later the same day, a statement was issued by the judiciary saying the ban on *Tous* had been lifted in the light of undertakings given by its managing director to make it less similar in appearance to *Jameah*.

Mayor Karbaschi has also appealed against his sentence. Meanwhile, a bank account has been opened to receive donations to pay Karbaschi's eventual fines. Donations have poured in. And the war continues. ❏

Nilou Mobasser is an Iranian writer and translator based in the UK

MOHAMMAD REZA ZA'ERI

When in doubt

The following excerpts from an interview with Hojjat ol-Eslam Mohammad Reza Za'eri, managing director of Khaneh *(House), appeared in the Tehran daily* Abrar *on 30 July 1998.* Khaneh *is the weekly journal of the House of Young Journalists. Its 'crime' is to have published a letter by a young girl on 15 July under the title 'No-one has time to reply'. The letter said, among other things, that Islam does not offer solutions to the problems of young people, that Khomeini's name brings to mind the horrors of the war with Iraq and that Khomeini's* fatwa *against Salman Rushdie made the world think of Iran as a terrorist country.*

The girl is said to have been a 12-year-old when Khomeini died and is, in many ways, representative of the post-revolution generation that constitutes around 70 per cent of Iran's population.

On 27 July, the House of Young Journalists was attacked with Molotov cocktails at 1.30am by unknown assailant. On 3 August, Za'eri appeared in court and was found guilty of publishing insulting material. But the press jury recommended leniency in view of the fact that he had expressed remorse and released him on bail prior to sentencing. On 6 August, the court pronounced: Khaneh's licence was revoked, Za'eri got a suspended sentence of six months and a Rial3m fine (US$1,000).

Abrar *Mr Za'eri, what's going on? We hear a great deal of talk these days against* Khaneh.

Za'eri We have a regular correspondence column in the paper. In the case in question, various personal concerns and religious matters are discussed between a young girl and a clerical figure. The whole thing goes back a few years to a time when a young girl confided her anxieties in an open and straightforward way to a learned man. ... Starting with the first letter and reply in 1375 [1996-97], we gradually published the entire correspondence following repeated requests from our readers.

In one of the letters, the cleric speaks about the personality of the late Imam [Khomeini] and the unprecedented grandeur of his spirit and, in her next letter, the youngster refers to her doubts and anxieties about the Imam. In the next issue the cleric answers her.

May, I clarify my own position. Not to mince words, the whole thing may have resulted from an error on our part. When we saw that by publishing an offensive letter without the response we had hurt the feelings of our boys who served at the front and the families of martyrs, we realised we had made a mistake in publishing the two in separate issues.

Why did you publish the question?

First, I think this is a problem faced by many youngsters who do not know the Imam. In other words, we have a gap or a rift between the generation that experienced the revolution and the post-revolution generation. We cannot ignore this. Even among religious and revolutionary families, there are children who have not understood the Imam and the revolution correctly and are not familiar with them.

Second, I believe that Shi'ism and the doctrine of the revolution and the culture of Imam Khomeini comprise a school of thought that involves asking questions and receiving answers. It involves debate and discussion and the exchange of ideas; it is based on reason. If a question is not raised, it cannot be answered. If there is no debate, there can be no satisfactory belief. We do not want to follow the tradition of official publicity, based on a contrived, official, administrative and government-oriented approach. We do not want to go down the same road as those school books that children angrily throw into a ditch at the end of the school year.

There are two sides to this matter. Yes, we made a mistake and, if we could go back we would not publish the piece in the way we did. We owe a serious apology to the *hezbollahi* nation, to martyrs' families to our combatants and to the leader [Khamene'i].

Having admitted that, however, how are we to raise religious and ideological problems? In my opinion, an idea must really penetrate into the hearts and minds of the people we are addressing: they must feel satisfied, they must accept something wholeheartedly. They must not fear to raise an objection because of our strength and influence, keeping silent, not expressing an opinion yet remaining in doubt to the depths of their souls. We must not deny there are problems, but have the courage and boldness to solve them. We must not console ourselves with the thought that the person we are addressing appears not to raise any objections and seems to accept what we are saying. If we are confident about the truth of our reply, we must not fear the onslaught of questions because we have firm and convincing answers. Our religion, ideology and school of thought is based on the idea that doubt is the starting point of certainty. We can see this approach in the behaviour of the Immaculate Imams [the 12 Shi'i Imams] and the noble Prophet who, even when a person expressed doubt about monotheism and the existence of God, declared, 'Have no fear; this is the beginning of certainty.'

Why should we, who are certain about the truth of what we believe, be afraid of facing questions and doubts, and why must we not allow a climate of debate and discussion? See how the eminent leader stresses that young people and university students must be interested in politics and debate. How can this come about if we do not allow thinking and debate? Some people are creating a situation now in which young people will be so afraid of the reaction they might arouse that they won't even consider discussing and debating things.

So you believe that everyone should be allowed to say whatever they like and insult everything openly?

Naturally, I'm not of the opinion that anything can be raised and aired. Religious, legal, ethical and conventional limitations exist everywhere and, for example, topics that can encourage immorality or insult sanctities or destroy religious principles are not permitted anywhere. ❏

Translated by Nilou Mobasser

CHRISTINE ANYANWU

Rats on two legs

The death of Nigerian dictator Sani Abacha released her from a 15-year jail term for reporting the news. Freedom does not take away the stain of conviction nor the fear next time

It was a journey that spanned 1,251 days. I moved 10 times through the nation's most notorious detention centres, through spooky, forsaken prisons. It was a tour of a world which, even in my worst nightmares, I could never have imagined. I had a taste of life at its most raw, perhaps its lowest and, in the process, got a fuller appreciation of human nature and our creator.

Kirikiri Women's Prison was the first prison I had seen in my life. I was led through the gate by 20 armed men in three trucks and two jeeps. The first whiff of air hit my nose, my stomach wrenched and I bent over and threw up in the reception hall. The thought of prison was abhorrent to every nerve in my body. It was mortifying enough to be tossed around in the Black Maria, but to be caged like an animal was devastating. By the time I got to the cell, all I wanted was close my eyes. I wished the night would draw on and on. For eight days I lived on bottled water. I had nightmares every night. Within eight days, my hair went grey.

Flip the scene. State security detention centre, Ikoyi. I am marooned in a huge building, locked in all day, drapes drawn, the room dark, dank, airless. My only neighbours are monstrous rats that not only hop, but actually walk on two legs. Now I hear the pounding in the wide, echo-filled hall as the heels of military shoes hit the cement floor with force. Minutes later I am in handcuffs and leg-chains.

Imagine a woman in a long tight skirt, arms cuffed, legs chained, attempting to climb a narrow, shaky ladder four feet high into an airless police truck. She is propped up by two soldiers while another 38 armed men surround the scene. Imagine, in the dark container, the vehicle speeding at 120mph, five other trucks blaring their sirens, the heavy Black Maria creaking thunderously with every bump, bounce or jerk. A sudden stop at a street light, and the bench slides in the opposite direction. I hit the floor, slide along and ram my head into the metal frame. We return after a 45-minute jolly ride round town. It is part of the breaking-down process.

The tribunal. Fifteen stiff men in uniforms sat on cushioned chairs on a raised platform. Ten uniformed men stood at strategic corners of the hall, automatic weapons in their arms. I sat on a bench facing the high table. Leg irons removed, I could at least cross my legs. In 30 minutes flat, Patrick Aziza, chairman of the tribunal, said he was giving me life imprisonment for being an 'accessory after the fact of treason'. It was the first time I had ever heard of such a crime. How did I become an accessory to a treasonable crime after it was committed? By publishing news of a coup in my weekly magazine, *TSM*.

Before and during this sham, I was denied contact with the outside and not permitted to invite my lawyer. A military man just out of law school was imposed on me. He was not permitted to contact my staff, relatives or anyone who could help my case. No witnesses were allowed. He was not permitted to visit me. We met at the tribunal. In the first few minutes of his presentation, the judge advocate threatened him with a court marshal. He crawled into his shell and let his superior officers have their way.

The Story. In March 1995, there was widespread speculation of an imminent coup d'état. Coups are big news in Nigeria because, in 38 years of independence, it has been the traditional mode of power succession. Coups jolt society. They reorder the affairs of the nation and the individual. There is no greater, more compelling 'new and urgent matter of public debate' than a coup. In the 1995 coup scare, the weight of the story was elevated more by the status of the individuals arrested. It was, therefore, a matter of compelling duty to the public to publish.

As we began to investigate the story, I received a telephone call from an official ordering me not to publish 'if you love your children'. But there was no 'pressing social need' to suppress the story. On the contrary, there was a compelling need to inform the public of what was happening.

In a news-breaking situation such as this, every journalist calls up his or her contacts. Contacts are assets in journalism, not a crime. *TSM*, like other publications, employed all legal avenues to get to the heart of the story, and this included talking to military men, government people, civilians and relatives of suspects.

It was, therefore, rather amazing when the Aziza military tribunal claimed that I was 'instructed' to publish the stories by one of our sources who happened to be a distant relative of one of the accused. Nothing could persuade them that a news source does not dictate the story. Put simply, I went to prison for 1,251 days for interviewing a stark, illiterate man, barely able to communicate, since he spoke only his native language. This in an effort to give our readers a true and accurate picture.

To muddy the waters, they fabricated a story suggesting that one of the accused plotters had a financial interest in our company and we, therefore, wrote about the coup to help him escape justice. The accusation was baseless since neither the man, nor anyone remotely connected with him, even held shares. But in any case, no law stops any Nigerian citizen from investing in private-sector enterprises and, if he had been an investor, nothing stopped the magazine from covering news of such overwhelming public concern. No one imprisoned the editors of the Concord Group for covering the ordeal of its proprietor, the late Abiola.

I was faced with a situation in which military men wanted to redefine journalism, dictate to me how I was to gather my information and how I was to write my story. I would not stand for that. What was clear was that Abacha and his team saw women as the weakest link in the chain of humanity and, therefore, put the squeeze on me to break the media chain. The cheap blackmail they fabricated was meant to pull the wool over the eyes of the fickle-minded who would believe any story. Incidentally, they could not find a convenient blackmail against my male colleagues Kunle Ajibade, Ben-Charles Obi and George Mba. But they imprisoned them just the same, using my case as a benchmark for the trial of all journalists.

TSM was not the only publication to run stories of the coup-scare. All other magazines and newspapers, except those with links with the regime, published. No other editor is known to have been overtly threatened in the manner I was. It was a sexist act of intimidation, another in a series of measures, including the forgery and printing of fake editions of *TSM* by Abacha's agents, aimed at scaring me off mainstream journalism.

What was at issue was the right of the individual to hold a non-violent thought, express a non-violent opinion. Abacha's position was that no-one had the right to call his acts into question and he demonstrated it amply throughout his administration. The landscape is littered with his victims who suffered solely for exercising their freedom of thought, freedom of speech or freedom of choice.

I was merely one of the earlier victims. I held dissenting views. That was a crime in his eyes. The coup was a convenient 'package' for silencing foes and dissenters. I was programmed into it. Without doubt, I suffered unwarranted punishment and a terrible insult. I am not bitter. I only hope that future generations of journalists are spared the same fate.

Although the new Abubakar regime has shown good sense in releasing journalists and other political prisoners, fear of media repression is far from gone. One significant way of putting this fear to rest would be to expunge the stain of the convictions from the records of innocent journalists. Journalists do not plan coups, they do not carry them out. They write about them.

There is a world of difference - and 1,251 days - between an observer and an actor. ❏

Christine Anyanwu was editor-in-chief and publisher of the weekly The Sunday Magazine. *The paper folded while she was in prison*

An International Quarterly
of the Social Sciences

Since 1934, **Social Research,** *an international, interdisciplinary quarterly, has published articles on the social sciences and the humanities by over 2,000 authors from throughout the world.*

Recent issue themes and selected authors:

Volume 64

The Decent Society   (64:1 Spring 1997)
Avishai Margalit, Steven Lukes, Anthony Quinton, Amélie Oksenberg Rorty

Nonthematic   (64:2 Summer 1998)
Richard Sennett, Nicholas Humphrey, Teresa Brennan, Timur Kuran

Technology and the Rest of Culture   (64:3 Fall 1997)
Arno Penzias, Leo Marx, John Hollander, Sherry Turkle

The Future of the Welfare State   (64:4 Winter 1997)
Guy Standing, Ethan Kapstein, Zsuzsa Ferge, Jacek Kochanowicz

Volume 65

Garbage   (65:1 Spring 1998)
Russell Hardin, Marian Chertow, Michael Thompson, Allen Hershkowitz

Taxonomy and Deviance   (65:2 Summer 1998)
Gilbert Herdt, John Dupré, Sander Gilman, Virginia Dominguez

Conversation   (65:3 Fall 1998, forthcoming)

Volume 66

Food: Nature and Culture (66:1); Hope and Despair (66:2); Prospects for Democracy (66:3); Positive and Negative Liberalism(66:4)

Orders

Annual subscription (within U.S.): Individuals $30, Libraries/Institutions $80
Single issue: Individuals $7.50, Libraries/Institutions $20.00. Prepayment required.
Send checks drawn against a U.S. bank in U.S. funds or VISA/MC number to:

Social Research, The New School for Social Research
65 Fifth Avenue, Room 354, New York, NY 10003
Tel: (212) 229-5776   Fax: (212) 229-5476   socres@newschool.edu
www.newschool.edu/centers/socres

Social Research is a publication of the Graduate Faculty
of the New School for Social Research. Arien Mack, Editor.

JO GLANVILLE

Lines of attack

If you want to take the temperature of Arab-Israeli relations, a look at the cartoons that enliven the newspapers on the two sides is instructive

For a short time after the 1993 Oslo Accords that initiated the Palestine-Israel peace process, the everyday stereotypes of every Israeli as a hook-nosed Nazi and all Arabs as monstrous terrorists appeared to lose currency: the language of political cartoons softened.

But within less than a year, well before the euphoria of the peace process died, the mistrust resurfaced. When Yasser Arafat arrived in Gaza in 1994, right-wing Israeli cartoonists were still portraying him as a terrorist, while cartoons in the Arab press continued to characterise Israelis as fascist murderers. With the election of Binyamin Netanyahu as Prime Minister of Israel in May 1996 the old norms made a rapid comeback.

'There was a dramatic change when Netanyahu took over,' says Abdel Bari Atwan, editor of *Al-Quds Al-Arabi*, the London-based Arab daily. 'He revived the criticism and the old style of cartoons. He gave cartoonists the fuel to criticise Israel: their cartoons are a reflection of frustration in the Arab world with Netanyahu and the Oslo Accords.'

Last year, the Anti-Defamation League in New York published a report on anti-Semitic cartoons in the Egyptian press and took out a full-page advertisement in the *New York Times* calling on President Hosni Mubarak to stop the 'anti-semitic hate in Egypt'. The protest coincided with the Egyptian President's visit to Washington in March. Mubarak countered with a report from his ministry of information detailing attacks on Egyptian policy in the Israeli press. He publicly took particular exception to articles and cartoons in the *Jerusalem Post*: the newspaper was banned in Egypt two years ago when it was still edited by

David Bar Illan, now one of Netanyahu's closest aides.

Some imagery is common to cartoons on both sides of the divide. Each portrays the other as cold-blooded creatures – reptiles or marine animals. After the suicide bombing in the West Jerusalem market of Mahane Yehuda in August 1997, Arafat was drawn as an octopus, a knife in one tentacle, a bomb in another, while writing an appeal for world sympathy with a third. Israel frequently appears as a threatening snake, its skin marked with the Star of David. The dove of peace is another frequent motif in both Arab and Israeli cartoons, usually meeting a sticky end: over the years, it has been stabbed, shot, strangled, eaten and crushed to death.

The Arab press gives greater prominence to cartoons than its Israeli counterpart. Bari Atwan believes local censors take them less seriously than the printed word, thereby allowing cartoonists marginally more licence than journalists. 'It indicates how stupid the censors are,' he says. 'Even the illiterate can look at a cartoon and laugh.'

By contrast, veteran Israeli cartoonist Kariel Gardosh, better known as 'Dosh', reckons the influence of the cartoon in Israel has waned as literacy has increased. 'There was a time when simple black and white cartoons were the main source of political information for the public, when there were fewer Hebrew speakers than now,' he says. 'Cartoons played an important part in forming public opinion.'

Neither Arab nor Israeli cartoonists are able to enjoy the full licence of the satirist to mock the establishment. Cartoonists from both sides speak of the necessity of self-censorship. 'Israel is not quite an open society,' says Israeli cartoonist Dudu Gever. 'There are open wounds.'

Another Israeli cartoonist, Oleg, has the dubious distinction of managing to offend both Arabs and Israelis. Egypt's ministry of information included a number of his cartoons in its report on the Israeli press and these contributed to the banning of the *Jerusalem Post*. In 1993, Oleg was arrested for drawing what was judged to be an anti-semitic cartoon in a Russian-Israeli newspaper. Through an image of a rabbi in a prison watchtower, clutching a chicken behind his back, as he peers through binoculars and barks out the order 'forbidden', it mocked the tyranny of kosher laws. The charges against Oleg were later dropped.

For Arab cartoonists, the fate of the great Palestinian Naji al-Ali, murdered in London in 1987, remains a grim reminder of just how dangerous their profession can be, (examples of his work can be seen at *www.indexoncensorship.org/Cartoon/palestine/palestine.html*). Al-Ali attacked the PLO, Israel and Arab regimes indiscriminately and all, at one time or another, have been accused of his murder. Recent victims of censorship include the Lebanese cartoonist Elie Saliba, who was accused of defamation for a cartoon in *Al-Diyar* in which he questioned the independence of the judiciary. The Committee to Protect Journalists has complained to the Lebanese government about its use of criminal defamation statutes to prosecute journalists. Saliba faces up to two years' imprisonment and a possible fine of US$66,000.

Amid the mutual recriminations of racism and anti-semitism, the diversity in Middle East cartoons tends to be overlooked. Hasib al-Jasim's cartoons in *Al-Quds Al-Arabi* offer sharp political commentary while George Bahgory's cartoons in *Al-Ahram Weekly* are unique, avant-garde creations. Bahgory, an Egyptian, is one of the most celebrated of all contemporary Arab cartoonists. Blacklisted by Sadat for satirising the Camp David accords, he has lived abroad for 15 years and still prefers to be based in Paris, out of the eye of the storm. He has his own 'rules of the road' when it comes to drawing Israelis: he never, for instance, uses the Star of David, commonly used to identify Israelis in Arab cartoons. 'I

Credit: Hasib al-Jasim/Al-Quds Al-Arabi

tell other Arab cartoonists that it is a form of racism,' he says. 'The star is not a political symbol, it is religious, and I respect every religion.'

Israel's most famous cartoonist, Ze'ev, who works for the newspaper *Ha'aretz*, has no time for the standard stereotypes. During the Iraq–UN crisis in February this year, he satirised the widespread tendency to portray Saddam Hussein as a monster. In one cartoon, he drew Israel as a child in bed, being frightened out of its wits by granny's nightmare stories of big, bad Saddam. In another, Bill Clinton, dressed as a soldier, blows a bugle while the world looks out of the window in alarm and Saddam appears on the horizon, fangs protruding from his mouth and a forest of missiles behind him. The Palestinian Khalil Abu Arafeh, cartoonist for *Al-Quds* in East Jerusalem, rarely draws Israelis and, when he does, sticks to politicians – he is unable to get his drawings of Israeli civilians and soldiers past the censor. 'There are a lot of types in Israel – settlers, soldiers, Haredim (ultra-orthodox Jews) – and when I draw them there may be stereotypes,' he says. 'The Israelis are sensitive to this. Anyone who draws them in this way may be accused of anti-semitism.'

A spokesman for the Israel Defence Forces said the only consideration for censorship is whether a cartoon threatens the security of Israel. Fifty years after independence, Tel Aviv still bases its censorship code on the emergency laws of the old British Mandate. Between the severity of the Israeli military censor and the intimidation of the Palestinian National Authority, Palestinian cartoonists in East Jerusalem are in an impossible position. If Khalil Abu Arafeh draws Yasser Arafat in anything other than a positive light, he can expect trouble. Arafat's intimidation of the local press has included banning newspapers and arresting journalists.

Cartoonists have responded enthusiastically to plans for a master-class for Middle East cartoonists hosted by the University of Malta this autumn. It will bring together Arab and Israeli cartoonists and is an attempt to address the 'war by other means' conducted in the press. But if the impasse in Arab-Israeli relations continues, participation may be a problem for some. One Arab who attended an exploratory meeting for media professionals in the Middle East earlier this year was publicly attacked on his return home for 'fraternising with Israelis', including finding himself on the receiving end of the cartoonist's pen. ❏

Jo Glanville is a freelance journalist living in London

His nose precedes him like a spear, albeit one damaged by his opponents' arrows; his eyes are hidden in
the murky waters of Israeli politics. Beneath those
heavy brows, however, they gleam like a crocodile's
teeth. His mouth is small and tightly closed, as befits
a man in his position. Ehud Barak says little, but he
sees the whirlpool swirling around him.

Credit: George Bahgory / Al-Ahram Weekly

EuroMedia

'We make the news; we decide what you shall — and most important shall not — hear.' For all its talk of greater transparency and accountability, the European Union has done little to honour those promises. Brussels is more given to withholding than releasing information and hounds journalists who try to get the story. Meanwhile, in the UK, a government that campaigned on the promise of freedom of information now threatens our right to know.

File compiled by Michael Griffin

MARTIN WALKER

Brussels spouts

Information overload, the exigencies of reporting on national interests, and the EU's reluctance to lift the curtain on its activities precludes most serious investigative journalism in the European capital

When Ronald Reagan came to Moscow in 1988 for the summit which declared that the Cold War was almost over, the White House correspondents were well briefed. They knew about Gorbachev and *glasnost* and the black market and the new 'No Smoking' rule on Red Square. The one feature of Soviet life that surprised them was the lavish facilities of the foreign press centre.

Since the 1980 Olympic Games, there had been a purpose-built hall for press conferences, complete with Russian-English simultaneous translation, a bar and, by Soviet standards, an unusually well-stocked restaurant. There was a work room with Russian and English typewriters, and upstairs were the offices of the Novosti press agency, where Soviet 'experts' were usually on hand for a cautious briefing.

'We have nothing like this in Washington,' marvelled CNN's Mary Tillotson, who enthralled the Moscow hands with a description of the old presidential swimming pool in the White House basement, which President Nixon had transformed into a press briefing room. She made it sound like the black hole of Calcutta; terribly cramped, no bar, no restaurant and hardly any telephones, where correspondents who were household names across the USA and whose incomes were counted in millions, squeezed daily into microscopic workspaces like mechanics sliding under a car.

When I arrived in Washington from Moscow in 1989, it was clear that she had not exaggerated. The White House briefing room was exactly that: a crude and functional podium for the daily briefing by the President's press secretary, several rows of cramped seats which were all reserved for the main US news outlets, and a platform for the massed regiments of TV cameras.

By contrast, when I arrived in Brussels from Washington in 1997, I felt for a moment that I was back in Soviet-era Moscow. There was a press centre in the basement of the Commission building with translation facilities and a small adjoining bar where all the gossip happened after the daily noon briefing. There was a work room, clean lavatories and stacks of written briefing notes provided fresh each day by the European Commission's press service. On Wednesdays, when the 20 Commissioners held their weekly meeting – and each has his/her own spokesperson with a departmental brief to peddle – they even provided free coffee in the bar and the sandwiches were about a third of the price you paid outside.

Across the road in the building of the Council of Ministers, or down the street in the lavish new Brussels centre of the European Parliament, it was just the same: briefings, spokesmen, bars, meeting rooms, phones and all material comforts. For the first few days, it seemed like journalism heaven after the reporting hell of the White House. But as one read the spokesman's notes and attended the daily Commission briefings, and each of the 15 national press briefings after each council session, a new rule of international journalism began to form: the greater the comfort, the less they have to say. The better they treat you, the more they have to hide.

Beyond the creature comforts of the hacks, there are further differences between the management of journalism in old Moscow and modern Washington. The most important is that despite the soundbite culture, in Washington they give answers. They have to. The US media functions in a doubly competitive environment. There are competing news outlets, four TV networks and three 24-hour TV news cable channels, weekly magazines, daily papers and the wires. That is the competition of demand. Just as important, because this is the essence of a pluralist society, there is competition of supply. The White House, the Congress and the State Department and big business and the think-tanks each have their own story to tell and their own spin to impart. One reason why *glasnost* was so important in Gorbachev's Moscow was that a kind of pluralism began to replace the official party line. There were alternative news sources, from traditional dissidents to the critical intellectuals, from the unofficial historians to the pro- and anti-*glasnost*, or pro- and anti-Yeltsin forces within the party machine.

Journalism in any major political centre is very largely about playing one source off against another, levering more information from X because Y and Z have already given you a part of the story. By this standard, Brussels functions rather well for journalists. Think of the place as if it were a copy of the US Constitution, in which the Parliament is the legislature, the Commission is the executive and the European Court of Justice is the judiciary. On top of that, Brussels offers the European Council, which is where the 15 national government meet to take the final political decisions. The Council has a bureaucracy of its own, but it is made up of 15 member states, each with its own embassy and its own press officer in Brussels, each determined to impart a national spin to the story of the day. And then there are all the non-governmental organisations, and that other institutional inhabitant of the city, the headquarters of the NATO alliance. All this guarantees competition of supply. The presence of over 2,000 accredited journalists in over 15 national media corps, plus international wire services and US and eastern European media, ensures competition of demand.

There is, however, a major difference. There is, so far, no such entity as the European media, and only the beginnings of a Brussels media to match that of Washington, or even of Moscow. If Brussels has a daily paper, it is the *Financial Times*, which devotes far more space than any other newspaper to its affairs. This is understandable, given the *FT*'s corporate readership whose businesses are often affected by Commission proposals or Council decisions, and given the extraordinary (and Brussels-led) development of the single currency. *Le Monde*, which used to play this role in the days when Europe meant the original six members, remains important. But published in Paris in the afternoons, it cannot begin to compete with the *FT* as a daily organ for Brussels. The *Economist* might claim to be the Brussels in-house weekly, except that its place has lately been usurped by its own stable-mate, *European Voice*, an intensely serious and Commission-focused tabloid weekly, written and published in and for Brussels. In Agence Europe, Brussels has its own daily news agency, whose long lists of unvarnished news reports of Commission statements are occasionally enlivened by the intensely Europhile signed editorials by its editor and part-owner, Ferdinando Riccardi.

But all these together do not begin to play the role of a *CNN, New*

York Times or *Washington Post* (nor of *Pravda* and TASS and the nightly Soviet TV news programme *Vremya*), as news organs which are the daily diet of everyone in the government-media-lobbying-corporate conglomerate of a superpower capital. Some of the gap is filled by Belgium's *Le Soir* and by the leading national papers of the major EU states, from the *Guardian* to *Le Figaro*, the *Daily Telegraph* to *Frankfurter Allegemeine Zeitung*, *The Times* to *Corriere della Sera*. The German weeklies *Der Spiegel* and *Focus*, and the French *L'Express* are also widely read, far more than the British-based weekly the *European*, which suffers from an editorial line that is perceived to be Eurosceptic. Brussels, in short, is a city without its own town cryer, a power centre that cannot hear itself think.

It is, therefore, a city in which the customary balance of power in a democracy between the rulers and the ruled does not hold. My colleagues on *Focus* magazine are all too well aware of the dangers of investigative reporting of an elite bureaucracy like the Commission, which does not see itself as answerable to anyone and which polices itself. This is made worse by the way the 15 national governments do not see their Council as a European institution, because with the deliberately enfeebled Parliament there is no real focus of European opinion to hold it to account. Playing to a national audience back home, they understandably offer a nationalist repertoire that ranges from stout self-interest to jingoism.

This may improve, now that the Treaty of Amsterdam requires 'transparency' in the way Europe is governed, and has given the Parliament a few more powers. Moreover, the new Labour MEP leader Alan Donnelly has cannily used the appointment of the first head of the European Central Bank to establish for Europe's Parliament the precedent of US Congress-style confirmation hearings. But for the moment, much of the reporting of the European capital would be more familiar to Mikhail Gorbachev than it would to Ronald Reagan. ❏

Martin Walker is the Guardian's *Brussels correspondent. He has represented the paper in Moscow and Washington*

Behind the lines

On 10 June this year, the EU Commission spokesman announced in the noon briefing that because of a European Court of Justice decision, 'the Commission has begun to verify the situation of budget lines without a legal basis and temporarily suspended their execution'. That was it. Despite spirited questioning, the Commission refused to say how much public money was involved, nor what programmes were at risk.

The following day, the *Guardian* was alone in reporting that £261 million (US$400 million) was in question, and the programmes at risk included all NGO work in the developing world, the EU's social budget for the disabled, the blind and pensioners, minority language broadcasts and services, and the campaign to ban landmines. None of the NGOs, from Oxfam to Médecins Sans Frontières, knew what was about to hit them. Senior Commission officials, warned that they could be held personally liable for improperly spent funds, turned off the computers to stop cheques from being sent out. The bureaucracy was thrown into chaos.

The story was obtained by asking one Commission official, in the social fund area which looked likely to be hard hit, what it meant. That obtained enough information to lever the full hit–list of threatened projects from another official in the budget department. Equipped with the list, the *Guardian* invited social affairs Commissioner Padraig Flynn to comment on the record; he said, 'This is a mortal challenge to the human face of Europe that we keep talking about.' Citing that statement, the *Guardian* then invited budget Commissioner Erkki Liikanen to comment; he said the law had tied his hands even though 'many of these programmes are ones I want personally to support'.

The court judgement came from a lawsuit filed by Britain, with the backing of the Council, after the previous Tory government had objected to the legal basis of the EU social fund spending £200,000 (US$300,000) on the rehabilitation of prostitutes in Bilbao and Vienna. The court then ruled that the entire social budget, which had been financed for over 20 years with broad but not specific authority from the Council and Parliament, was being spent improperly. The new British government spokesman told the *Guardian* that it 'does not feel any great guilt – taxpayers' money has to be accountable'.

The labyrinthine architecture of Brussels – Credit: Rex/Lehtikuva

Under intense pressure from NGOs and European MEPs, who extracted a promise to resolve the matter from Prime Minister Tony Blair when he visited the European Parliament in Strasbourg, the Commission and the British government, in its role as holder of the presidency of the Council, strained every nerve to repair the damage. They set new Brussels records in passing legislation to restore almost all the budget authority by the end of July.

They might have done so anyway. But without the *Guardian*'s report, they would have been under no pressure to do so, and the public would never have known a thing. ❏

MW

Corruption and the Commission

These six blank pages replace an article we planned to publish on internal corruption in the European Commission, written by an experienced and respected journalist. Such have been the kafkaesque obfuscations in the EC, and such has been the pressure on the journalist concerned, that *Index* finally felt unable to expose him to further risk.

Index has reported for 26 years on the harrassment of journalists and official cover ups all over the world. It is easy enough for us to protest at these violations of free expression when they occur in Nigeria, in Burma, in Turkey. But some of these things are happening in our own backyard. Open and objective discussion of corruption or mismanagement in the EC is virtually impossible. In as far as we are able, we are giving our readers an idea of what some of the issues are.

In June this year the European Court reported: 'There are recognised cases, for instance tourism, where files were withheld from UCLAF investigators [the anti-corruption agency that reports only to the Commission] and incriminating documents were systematically destroyed.'

MEP Rosemarie Wernheuer, a German corruption expert, criticised the EU for protecting officials and for paying lawyers representing officials under investigation to hound journalists critical of its goings on. She found it 'legally reprehensible that the EU should decide for itself whether the law should apply to its own officials.'

Reimer Boge, German Christian Democrat representative on the investigative committee of the European Parliament, said that the Commission had 'neglected to cooperate' in the inquiry into the BSE affair. 'The Commission hampered the work of this committee by not disclosing, or deliberately locking away, important documents.'

A libel action is being brought by Commission officials against the German magazine *Focus* for reporting a financial scandal, alleged by internal auditors, in the EC. The plaintiffs are demanding the equivalent of US$1 million in damages. Their legal costs are being funded with EU taxpayers money by the Commission.

Figures released by the European Court of Auditors reveal 40 recent cases of internal corruption, nepotism or mismanagement. EU officials enjoy legal immunity. The EU alone decides whether there is sufficient evidence to mount a prosecution against an official. ❑

DUNCAN CAMPBELL

Listening in silence

On the twentieth anniversary of the UK's notorious 'ABC' secrecy trial, one of the defendants exposes the Anglo-Saxon Trojan horse that keeps an ear tuned to Europe from secret bases in the UK and breaks the spirit, if not the letter, of the UK's treaty agreements with the European Union

During the first half of 1998, continental Europe's press reported extensively on the scale of US and British electronic spying within Europe. Italy, Spain, France, Germany, Scandinavia and the Netherlands enjoyed front-page coverage of a system called Echelon, a global computer espionage network run by the UK intelligence organisation Government Communications Headquarters (GCHQ), and its US counterpart, the huge National Security Agency (NSA). This autumn, the issue of US electronic espionage in Europe will come before the Council of Ministers. But the UK press has been almost completely silent.

The issues being debated abroad point to a political schizophrenia that still afflicts the UK's political establishment. Are we Europeans or Atlanticists? Have we adapted to a new world order, with humanitarian priorities to the fore, or is the new order merely the 'American order'? Where intelligence is concerned, the answer is assuredly the latter. Within Europe, however, the core issue is whether the 'Anglo-Saxon' intelligence stations located in Britain are being used to spy on mainland commerce and politics, either for the benefit of the US and UK – or even the US alone.

A former chief of GCHQ, Sir Leonard Hooper, once famously wrote to his US counterpart that the sheets around the bed in which both lay were tucked in so tight that the relationship was better than their respective governments enjoyed. Those words were written 30 years ago;

their truth endures to this day.

What few realise, even in the supercharged debate led by papers like Italy's *Il Mondo*, is that they are only belatedly discovering systems that have been embedded in the core of our social infrastructure – the communications systems – for 50 years. Echelon is only the latest embodiment of secret listening systems that have spanned the globe since the 1940s, augmented more recently by listening satellites positioned in space.

For 30 years after World War II, the very existence of the UK/US electronic intelligence system was completely unknown. Until the 1970s, the wall of secrecy which surrounded global systems of 'signals intelligence', or 'sigint', was fiercely enforced. The first chink appeared in 1972 when a former NSA employee, Winslow Peck, wrote an exposé for the radical US magazine *Ramparts*. In 1973, a brief glimpse of

GCHQ Cheltenham was excised from an ITN *World in Action* TV documentary under the 'D-Notice' system. In 1976, I wrote the first ever account of GCHQ for the London entertainment guide, *Time Out*.

'in the decade since the Cold War ended, the network is still being enlarged'

The direct consequence of that revelation was the 'ABC case', a two-year trial ending in 1978 in which I and two other defendants faced charges under the Official Secrets Act that could have resulted in 30 years' imprisonment. Peck, who assisted in the report, was banned for ever from British shores. The co-author Mark Hosenball, another American, was deported from the UK, along with the ex-CIA radical writer Philip Agee.

These early exposés have long been superseded. They also contained omissions and led to errors of understanding. In 1972 Peck had described how the system of intelligence surveillance was centred on 'keywords'. These were names of people, organisations and subjects of current intelligence interest. Prominent among them were the leaders of Third World radical movements; Robert Mugabe and Samora Michel were two. Collectively, the keywords belonged to a 'watchlist' that the NSA and GCHQ analysts used to separate the interesting from the mundane.

Re-reporters of Peck's revelations interpreted what he said as applying to all telephone calls which, they reported, could automatically be scanned for words of interest without human intervention. Although this must certainly be the case now, it took more than 20 years for it to become a reality. Peck's revelations of automated keyword-spotting related then only to machine communications, such as telex and telegrams.

The origins of this system go back to World War II and the allied codebreaking effort. A global eavesdropping network was reconstituted in 1947 and 1948. It was anticipated that electronic monitoring of communications signals would continue to be the most important form of post-war intelligence-gathering, as it had been throughout the war. The English-speaking powers – the US, UK, Canada, Australia and New Zealand – signed a secret agreement on 'sigint'.

Called Ukusa (UK-USA), the agreement assigned parts of the globe to each participating agency. GCHQ Cheltenham coordinates operations for Europe, Africa and the former Soviet Union west of the Ural

Mountains. NSA covers the rest of the Soviet Union and most of the Americas. Australia – where another listening station is located – monitors the South Pacific and South East Asia.

Only a handful of civil servants and a few ministers in each participating country are allowed to know what is done, whose interests are served, or to look at or evaluate Echelon's 'product'. Everything is hidden behind a network of codewords to which access is only permitted after 'indoctrination'. In the decade since the Cold War ended, the network is still being enlarged. The scale of clandestine information-gathering raises fundamental questions about national security, conflicting commercial interests and personal privacy.

In the context of government and citizen, the largest questions arise from Echelon's mission to spy on international civil and commercial communications. Unnoticed at the time, the network has been monitoring all the West's communications before and since the first large satellites, called Intelsat, went into orbit at the start of the 1970s. Simultaneously, the spy partners built satellite ground stations (Britain's is in Cornwall) to harvest and analyse all that Intelsat carried. None of those communications were from the Soviet Union or its allies, far less its military forces or their commanders.

It took a long time after the first revelations about GCHQ and NSA for anyone to appreciate how much of their spying was directed at civilian traffic and not the diplomatic and military communications of actual or potential enemies. Within the intelligence world, the group of civilian targets had a name: International Leased Communications, or ILC.

Glimpses first emerged of ILC surveillance around 1970. In 1968, the *Daily Express* revealed that copies of international telegrams were being collected every day by unmarked van and taken to a secret office in Westminster. GCHQ was not mentioned, but it resulted in a political storm over the effectiveness of the 'D-Notice' system, used by the government to gag the media when, it claims, defence interests are threatened. The story was repeated in the USA in the first years after Watergate. Congressional investigators learned the NSA was receiving daily deliveries of copies of all overseas telegrams from New York and other locations under projects codenamed Shamrock and Minaret.

Nobody drew any connections between the two projects. Nevertheless, the London vans of the 1960s and the Shamrock project in the 1970s were the contemporary equivalent of Echelon. The differences are only of scale and technology. In 1972, telegrams were sent – and secretly copied – on paper. Human analysts read them and passed them on. During Watergate, it was revealed that NSA, in collaboration with GCHQ, had routinely intercepted the communications of prominent anti-Vietnam war leaders, such as Jane Fonda and Dr Benjamin Spock. Another target was former Black Panther leader Eldridge Cleaver.

In the Echelon computer network, interception and analysis is done automatically, through global networks of computers that can sit and sift, unattended. Literally millions of communications are now intercepted every hour. The watchlists and the human analysts are no more; they have been replaced by workhorse computers named, not inappropriately, Dictionary. Dictionary computers are programmed remotely with users' requirements for communications intercepts.

One of the UK's major Echelon stations is the interception base at Bude in Cornwall. If its computers are tasked to locate intelligence and pass it on to some latter-day Colonel Oliver North to help make mayhem in Central America, no-one in the UK will know. By 1992, according to a former director of the NSA, the system was selecting and processing two million intercepted messages every hour. The total will be vastly greater now. In London, a Dictionary system is installed on the top floor of offices at Palmer Street near Scotland Yard. These are the London offices of GCHQ.

Who are they listening to? According to a stream of revelations by intelligence workers in the 1980s and 1990s, the list included Scottish trade unionist Campbell Christie; Third World charities such as Oxfam; businessmen such as Tiny Rowland and Robert Maxwell; major UK and international corporations; and top Catholic figures, including European archbishops, the Pope and Mother Teresa.

One perspective on the sigint agencies plans came to light in the UK three years ago. Women peace campaigners at the NSA's intelligence base at Menwith Hill, near Harrogate, obtained a haul of papers from inside the base. These included a valedictory despatch to NSA staff from their outgoing director, Admiral William Studeman. He lamented how the end of the Cold War had swept away much of the intelligence community's *raison d'être*. But the NSA was determined, he wrote, not just to carry on, but to expand: 'Target technology will be tough. Many outsiders will want to rationalise a reduced threat dimension in order to further decrement intelligence for alternative agendas, [but] the demands for increased global access are growing.'

The frontiers of the information age are different from traditional alliances. But for those with the power to listen in, there are no frontiers. Nor may they rely on the press to be vigilant. The nature and existence of the Echelon network was first revealed in the *New Statesman* magazine a decade ago. The report described how Echelon, also known as Project P415, was being planned as the global surveillance system for the 1990s. No-one paid attention. The revelation that is finally on Europe's front pages was not reported then in Britain nor anywhere else.

Some years afterwards, a researcher in the furthest flung member state of the sigint alliance struggled to uncover what New Zealand's role in Echelon might be. Nicky Hager, a peace researcher with a background in physics, was tantalised in 1988 when the defence minister revealed that two intelligence stations being built in Australia and New Zealand were to be targeted on communications satellites used by Third World countries such as India and Indonesia. The Australians were furious at the slip-up, but the cat was out of the bag. Over the next years, Hager put together more information about Echelon and the 1990s electronic espionage system than anyone before or since. The result was a 250-page book, *Secret Power*.

Hager describes Echelon as an 'automated international surveillance system' that integrates secret monitoring stations across the globe using the intelligence agencies' own network of satellites and listening bases. At each base, Echelon Dictionaries automatically search through intercepted messages according to target lists of subjects and people. The key significance of the new system is that before Echelon, different countries and different stations knew what was being intercepted and to whom it was being sent. Intercepts were processed and checked before it was released. Now, even security cleared operators may not know what raw information is being sent out, or to whom.

Dictionary computers hold lists of the different categories of intercept available on the system, each identified by a four-digit code. Targets in the South Pacific include Japanese and French diplomatic messages, regional communications and the activities of Russian fishing boats and Antarctic bases. According to operators, Dictionary search results appear 'almost instantaneously'.

In 1992, the former NSA chief stated that the system was processing two million intercepts every hour. According to Hager, the New Zealand intelligence agencies only analysed 2,000 messages a week. An un-named Echelon operator in New Zealand told him that while the Americans have access to everything collected by its allies, they do not share all their information. 'The [intelligence] agencies can all apply for numbers on each other's Dictionaries. The hardest to deal with are the Americans. [There are] more hoops to jump through, unless it is in their interest, in which case they'll do it for you.'

In the foreword to *Secret Power*, former Prime Minister of New Zealand David Lange wrote that its revelations came as a complete surprise to him, despite his having been the premier who allowed the project to go ahead. He had authorised the construction of the monitoring station in a bid to limit the isolation inflicted on New Zealand by the USA and UK after his declaration of the country's 'nuclear free zone' policy in the mid-1980s. But he had no idea that thereby 'we had been committed to an international integrated electronic network.'

Hager uncovered details of the spy station at Blenheim, in an isolated wine-producing region on South Island. It was locked onto a commercial communications satellite, Intelsat 701, that started operations in January 1994. The small Pacific islands were among its targets, as were Japanese commercial and diplomatic messages. A few months after publishing his book, Hager and a TV reporter made a remarkable trip into the station itself, passing sensors and cameras undetected. Late at night they filmed through partly-curtained windows. The manuals they filmed on the supervisor's desk were the operating instructions for Intelsat satellites.

Their second discovery was almost iconic in terms of intelligence in the information age. Although the station's operations room held rows of computers, they functioned unmanned. They were analysing the whole communications pulse of the Pacific, but no-one was there. Instead, the Dictionary system sifted what was heard, passing it on automatically to such customers as the CIA and the Pentagon.

It was not until two years later that Hager's revelations drew other than local attention. In 1997, British researcher Dr Steve Wright was preparing a report on the technologies of political control for an obscure subcommittee of the European Parliament called Science and Technology Options Assessments. His lengthy report contained only a few paragraphs on the power of Echelon. But after it was presented to the European Parliament, the EU's nerve of awareness finally twitched.

To date in the UK, New Labour's ministers have maintained the past tradition of silence on all these issues. The position will become more difficult to hold when continental European counterparts challenge them on the issue of providing the USA with territory on which to site facilities such as the Menwith Hill station. Third World charities, resistance leaders and environmental organisations are not appropriate targets for an espionage architecture created for the Cold War. As human rights in the information age comes to depend more and more on information privacy, it is time for the espionage dinosaurs to retreat.

But they are advancing. ❏

Duncan Campbell, formerly the chairman and associate editor of the New Statesman, *is an investigative reporter and independent television producer*

urgent: support free access to the British Library

At the beginning of July the Board of the British Library released its *Strategic Review Consultation Paper* to the general public. The *Consultation Paper* estimates that in the immediate future the Library will suffer a funding shortfall of £20 million per annum. To guard against this the Paper recommends the introduction of a £300 per annum readers fee.

On 28 August the consultation process launched by the Board of the British Library will draw to a close, well in advance of the return of most students and academics from their summer break. There must be many journalists, scholars and other interested parties who will be surprised and alarmed that this document was made available for such a short period, at a time when many academics will not have seen it.

An Emergency Committee was set up at the beginning of August to protest against any charges on principle. It is the feeling of the Campaign that Brian Lang, the Chief Executive, and the Board have acted in a manner calculated to minimise public discussion of its unprecedented proposal of charging for access to what is the country's – arguably the world's – greatest *public* library. As Peter Ackroyd recently pointed out, had such a charge operated in the past, Karl Marx, H.G.Wells, Dickens, Shaw, George Gissing, and Ackroyd himself are among those who would have been prevented from producing much of the literature that has made the Library the incomparable resource it has become.

We urge everyone who is concerned about this issue to acquire and respond to the *Consultation Paper* as soon as possible, even if the 28 August deadline has passed (it can be accessed on the web at www.bl.uk/information/strat-bs.html). In addition, please make your views known to your own MP and to Chris Smith, the Culture Secretary.

For any further information on the Campaign, please call 0171 249 9592

Campaign to Keep the British Library Free

NICK COHEN

Go for the full monty, Tony!

**In opposition, freedom of information was at the front of
Labour's vision; in power, myopia has taken hold**

For a party whose policies are tailored to snake snugly round every
bulge and crevice of bourgeois prejudice, New Labour retains the
ability to flummox its critics with prolier-than-thou invective. It
condemns the cause of turning the British from subjects of Elizabeth II,
her heirs and successors, into citizens with a right to find out what is
done to them in their name with their money, in the language of what
was known in the bad old days as the politics of envy. Freedom of
information is an issue which merely stirs the elitist minds of the
'chattering classes', said Jack Cunningham, the government's new policy
coordinator. It appealed only to 'Chianti drinkers' lounging in their
Tuscan holiday villas, an anonymous Labour MP told the *Financial Times*.
Who cares apart from 'middle class wankers?' asked Alastair Campbell,
the Prime Minister's eloquent spokesman. Real, decent people couldn't
give a damn.

It was not always thus. In March 1996, a little over a year before he
came to power, Tony Blair was the middle classes' most spirited onanist.
A severe case of Portnoy's complaint propelled him into declaring that a
Freedom of Information Act was not one priority among many for the
coming Labour government but 'a change that is *absolutely* fundamental
to how we see politics developing in this country over the next few
years'. Destroying official secrecy would encourage 'disillusioned' voters
to trust him and end their 'disaffection' with leaders. New Labour
wanted to end state censorship because it was concerned with 'genuinely
changing the relationship in politics today'.

Trust was then Blair's watchword. For his liberal-left supporters it was a soundbite with paradoxical consequences. After four election defeats the electorate had to trust him not to reverse Conservative tax and spending policies. But after the Major administration had sunk in a septic tank of scandal, voters must also be able to trust New Labour to be honest, clean and, above all, open. Those who could barely stomach Blair's accommodation with Thatcherism were consoled by the thought that he would at least begin the overdue task of exposing the workings of an imperial British state, which had lost an Empire but found the role of keeping its last uppity natives in the dark congenial and essential. Blair appeared to recognise Whitehall's colonial attitudes toward the supposedly – although not legally – sovereign people. As his speech to an audience of constitutional reformers reached its climax, he said official secrecy was 50 years out of date. It was abhorrent to an increasingly educated and demanding populace. It ensured incompetence and worse went unpunished. The modern leader promised to sweep secrecy aside and allow politics 'to catch up with the aspirations of people by delivering not just more open but more effective and efficient government for the future'.

As I write in the summer of 1998, 15 months into the Labour government, the chances of a robust Freedom of Information Act becoming law range from the slim to the microscopic. There may well be a bill presented to Parliament with the the words 'freedom', 'information' and 'of' somewhere in its title, but the paltry measure will give the appearance of openness while keeping the secret culture in place.

Cynical wisdom holds that no party willingly disseminates information that was once secret after it has experienced the joys and burdens of office. Freedom of information is a measure it delivers within months of winning an election or not at all. And indeed, the corruption of power is part of the explanation for Labour's apostasy, but so, too, is the corruption of defeat. The arguments of those willing to fight for *glasnost* – whose number, encouragingly, includes at least 200 backbench MPs – will be strengthened if we look at how and why the bill is being neutered.

In the same month Blair gave his passionate speech, Peter Mandelson was telling quite a different story to a seminar organised by the Campaign for Freedom of Information. The passing of an act 'may have to wait', he said. Mandelson was 'extremely cautious' about revealing civil servants' advice to ministers. Good politicians were the answer to demands for transparency. Mere laws could not provide a substitute for ministers who behave 'with integrity and with honesty and openness'.

The paternalist view of the old establishment could not have been put better. The system works, in general, Mandelson implied. Criticism should be directed at the odd rotten apple and change confined to replacing tired old Conservatives with honest New Labour. The need is for a legal right to know, which can be exercised by citizens regardless of whether the government is good or bad or – as so often – indifferent to their interests.

Mandelson's influence has become so great he has turned the label 'control freak' from an insult from the hippy fringe to the cliché of choice for lazy mainstream pundits. His dominance of the Party's presentation and, by extension, its policies (in the end style and content are one) was only possible because Labour's run of defeats left it willing to do anything to stop the often far-right and largely foreign-owned press from tearing it apart again.

The tight little tactics of agenda manipulation and black propaganda continued into government. New Labour special advisers, whose only skill is in spinning on behalf of their masters, have replaced permanent civil servants as the most significant members of Whitehall departments. The party has lobbied editors to fire 'unhelpful' journalists. In at least one case, they were successful. Paul Routledge, a reporter loathed by the Blairites, had the offer of the political editorship of the *Daily Express* withdrawn after pressure from Downing Street. Policy arguments in cabinet are becoming a distant memory. The average cabinet meeting lasts slightly longer than the average sit-com, although the quality of political debate can often be lower. Labour Party dissenters can have their seats taken from them by the leadership. Loyalists willingly receive instructions on what to do and say from the whips on their pagers. (One MP told me that four of his colleagues had refused to take part in a charity swim because it would mean removing their vibrating bleepers for an hour. I vainly studied his face for a hint he was joking.)

Many commented on the irony of such an anal party opening up government. Now the contradiction is being resolved. David Clark, the minister who was originally put in charge of freedom of information, was fired in the summer reshuffle. He had been subjected to a continuous campaign against him from brave, anonymous sources who whispered their criticisms to equally courageous political journalists. Clark believes that the open liberal position he defended in disputes with Mandelson was not the best career move. He did manage to produce a white paper before he was knifed which, although excellent in parts, had several glaring defects. Jack Straw, the Home Secretary, insisted that all information on the penal powers of the police and security, immigration and social services must be excluded from the bill. His victory ensured that basic information on policing – why a 999 call was not answered, how many officers were on duty at a football match – will be official secrets.

Straw was unrepentant. 'If you openly provide intelligence about the total number of police officers available, then that would be used by criminals,' he sternly told an audience of MPs, many of whom could not keep the mocking sneers from their lips. Even in the USA, the most punitive country in the developed (and in much of the Third) world, which sends 1.8 million people a year to its barbarous prisons, such information is freely available. But secrecy will remain in place in Britain to stem the ever-present menace of Russian organised crime, Colombian drug barons and British citizens with ideas above their station.

Straw confessed that the high office of Home Secretary instilled a natural bias against freedom of information. 'The Home Office deals with areas of very sensitive business. It is about law and order. National security. Keeping 63,000 people in prison who do not want to be there.' He was, he added, in a business with 'genuine secrets'.

Such sentiments, which owe as much to cheap thrillers as political realities, are shared by interior ministers across the world. They are not in themselves surprising. What was shocking was Straw being given the task of drawing up the openness act when Clark was dumped. The macho poses of Westminster's hardman will therefore determine how much liberty the state will allow. And from what we know of Straw, the few gains that Clark made could disappear.

One of the virtues of Clark's proposals, for example, was that outside the large world of law enforcement, information would only be censored if civil servants could prove that its release would cause 'substantial harm'. Yet in his evidence to the Commons, Straw gave strong hints that he preferred what is known, in the jargon of constitutional reform, as the 'simple harm test'. This restrictive definition, brought in by the previous Conservative government, allows bureaucrats to suppress documents when, in their considered view, and after all relevant factors have been taken into account, they could somehow, at an unspecified date in the future, just conceivably cause harm.

The full subtlety of the simple harm test was revealed when the Department of Health refused to release a copy of its guidelines on disability benefit to an inquiring member of the public. The book was classsifed as a confidential document even though it had been printed by Her Majesty's Stationery Office and was meant to be on open sale.

The culture Straw appears willing to defend encourages the state to regard those who ask questions of government as harmful and legitimate objects of surveillance. A leaked memo from the Health and Safety Executive darkly warned that Dr Charles Woolfson, a senior lecturer at Glasgow University, and three other thoroughly respectable researchers, were 'becoming persistent in their enquiries to HSE'. It continued: 'We wish to monitor those who appear to have an interest in a range of HSE's activities and who may be looking to exploit replies received in ways unfavourable to HSE.' Dr Woolfson's crime was to try to examine the failure of the HSE to investigate burnings, poisonings, amputations and blinding suffered by workers in the North Sea oil fields. In a flourish which can only be described as, if you will forgive the platitude, Kafkaesque, the HSE memo concluded by saying that 'any contact with these people should be reported to the Open Government Unit'. Thus open government becomes an instrument of control.

For the moment, it looks as if New Labour can get away with pretty much anything it wants. The opposition is hopeless and the bovine press is placid. A Freedom of Information Bill will not be presented to Parliament until 1999 at the earliest and, as we have seen, it may well be wastepaper. Yet Tony Blair's original insight was correct. This government is rapidly developing an unsavoury reputation as an untrustworthy group of hypocrites, marketing men and manipulators. The Prime Minister and Campbell ought to be able to see that a full Freedom of Information Act could silence their critics and counter an emerging stereotype that will one day, in my view, drive them from power. Their blind failure to act shows that the Victorian fears about the consequences of masturbation may not be pure superstition. ❏

Nick Cohen is a columnist for the Observer

Don't let the Government block Freedom of Information!

The Government is proposing to drop a Freedom of Information Act from the coming year's legislative programme. Any delay is likely to lead to a substantial watering down of the proposals. Yet FOI was a Labour manifesto pledge and the party has been committed to the reform for 25 years. Tony Blair said in 1996 that FOI was "*not some isolated constitutional reform*" but "*a change that is absolutely fundamental to how we see politics developing in this country over the next few years...It is genuinely about changing the relationship in politics today*". So why is it being blocked?

It's *your* right to know - insist on it! You can help by:

*   Writing to the Prime Minister at 10 Downing Street, London SW1A 2AA urging him to ensure that a Freedom of Information Bill is included in the next Queen's speech

*   Writing to your MP asking him or her to urge the government to introduce this vital legislation immediately

*   Learning more about the government's proposals by writing to us for an information pack or visiting our web site at *http://www.cfoi.org.uk*

*   Supporting the Campaign's work by sending us a donation.

Campaign for Freedom of Information
Suite 102, 16 Baldwin's Gardens, London EC1N 7RJ, UK
Tel: 0171 831 7477 Fax: 0171 831 7461
e-mail: admin@cfoi.demon.co.uk

ROBERT COCKROFT

A world of your own

Accountants and media pundits would say it's not cost effective, but the editor of a provincial paper in the north of England is proving them wrong. Demand for 'local' news is insistent and insatiable

Shortly after I arrived in the editor's chair at Yorkshire's *Barnsley Chronicle*, the World Association of Gremlins decided to hold a convention in our computer. Things looked bad, but not catastrophic. Enough stories had gone to the Macs to enable us to get a paper out. But a lot of district material was still stuck in the front-end system and no amount of technical syrup of figs could ease its constipation.

We publish seven broadsheet editions of the *Chronicle*. They range from the town edition – 22,000 copies – to the Dearne Valley edition – 1,000. Our total average weekly circulation is a whisker below 40,000. At about 4.00pm, with the system still down and reporters inputting stories with anything from PCs to hairdryers, we made a decision. We had enough material to go with three editions. They would get their own front pages. The other four would get the town front. At 6.00pm, when most of the pages would normally have gone, our technical manager roused the system from its coma.

If we hung on late, we might get some of the copy for our inside district pages. Those are the ones in seven point saying who was the sidesman at Evensong at St Damien's and who won the raffle at the Dog and Gun. The day had been fraught. We stuck to our plan. It turned out to be a bad decision. At 8.30 the following morning, the phones began to ring. Hand-delivered notes started to come in. By Monday, we had received nearly 400.

We all staffed the phones. Computer fault? Our readers seemed understanding. The following week, though, our return rate doubled. We lost about 1,000 copies. The previous week, coincidental with a three pence price increase, we had put on 1,000 by printing a supplement carrying pictures of every child starting in primary school in Barnsley. I learned more about market research in a couple of hours than from any number of seminars.

Here were committed readers telling us what they missed, what they expected, what they thought and how they felt. Above all, their complaints served to highlight the importance they attached to intensely local news; their dislike of abrupt, unannounced changes; and the danger of producing a paper that satisfies our own professional vanities, while neglecting the real interests of the reader

The greatest number of complaints came from Wombwell, a community with a strong tradition of local news, and it was also the edition that we were using as a template to develop other areas. One woman reader said the absence of the district pages had been the talk of the local coffee morning. Another asked whether we had changed our policy? 'We rely on you to tell us what's going on, what's gone on, where to go, what to do and generally what's what,' he said.

He wasn't talking about what was going on in Penistone or in Hoyland or in Barnsley, but in his neighbourhood. On his street. A few minutes earlier, I'd been debating with the chief sub whether a standfirst should be in 15 pt Garamond Book and whether we should squeeze the Frutiger by five per cent. Suddenly matters were brought into perspective.

The man had touched on one reason why I left a features executive job at the *Yorkshire Post* to go to Barnsley, where mining is history, unemployment is above the national average and educational attainment well below it. I was keen to see what could be learned at grass-roots level, not least because 'local news' seems always to head the list of what market researchers call 'essentiality' in newspapers. Local news, for us, means effort and detail. It means nurturing sources, it means downgrading the phone in favour of human contact. It means routine, foot-slogging, door-to-door news gathering. It means hunting the local exclusives then seeing their worth confirmed when they appear in the nationals. Our research tells us that readers get their international and national news elsewhere. So we don't bother with it. We give readers a world view, but it's of their own world.

General features on gardening, travel, cookery, fashion, finance, 'A Doctor writes': we chucked them all. People get that stuff elsewhere in reams. What they can't get is what's happening next door, across the road, down the street, in the pub, on the local recreation ground. Yes, we have a columnist, but he's an ex-miner and he's rooted and credible. Our newsdesk gives pushy London-based PRs nervous breakdowns. They simply can't understand that we haven't an atom of interest in what they are promoting.

We've still a long way to go, but consistently rising circulation over the past four years suggests that readers appreciate our obsessively local approach. We have more than 70 separate communities in our borough; that's how many districts our reporters and local correspondents regularly cover. We carry hundreds of small paragraphs each week about these places. But isn't this what weeklies, even evening papers, formerly did? I sometimes wonder if we are not so preoccupied with the management of change and innovation that we ignore what the past is saying.

One factor working against street news has been cost-cutting. This form of journalism is labour-intensive. I'm fortunate in working for an independent newspaper whose directors are supportive of our efforts to become even more local, more nailed to the communities we serve. They have invested in extra staff and it's paying off. Unlike larger groups who sacrifice local news to the short-term needs of shareholders, we can take a longer view.

When people from Bournemouth to Barnsley have read the same national agency story, rehashed 50 times by papers, magazines, interactive devices, local radio and TV, national broadcasters, cable, digital satellite, teletext and the worldwide web, they will value what is new and fresh and different and relevant and real. And much of it will be local. Community news. Parish news. Neighbourhood news. Street news. ❏

Robert Cockcroft became editor of the Barnsley Chronicle in 1994

JULIAN PETLEY

An unsavoury business

Fear of libel actions and of losing advertising revenue has persuaded most media organisations to leave well alone when it comes to exposing some of the more unsavoury aspects of the burger giant McDonald's

Do you know that Helen Steel and Dave Morris, the McLibel Two, are scheduled to start their appeal on 12 January 1999? Did you realise that the trial judge ruled in the defendants' favour in the case of two-and-a-half of their seven groups of allegations against McDonald's, and that these concerned cruelty to certain animals, exploitation of children via advertising and low pay? Were you actually aware of the trial throughout its record-breaking 314-day run? And, finally, have you heard that both the BBC and Channel 4 refuse to show the independently-produced documentary *McLibel: Two Worlds Collide*?

If your answer is 'no', it's not surprising. Although at the climax of this legal blockbuster the media were temporarily awash with 'David and Goliath' stories, all too often laced with unnecessary and patronising 'human interest' angles, the vast majority of this crucial libel trial received remarkably little coverage. As the McLibel Support Campaign state on their McSpotlight website: 'You would've expected the entire media to line up behind the defence, if only out of pure self-interest. But the media seem to treat McDonald's either with awe and sycophancy, or else as daft and jokey, a well-loved service organisation.' It was, to quote Michael Mansfield QC, as if a *'cordon sanitaire'* had been placed around the whole subject. It is still in existence.

Admittedly, McDonald's *is* a potentially tricky media subject. Firstly, as the McLibel case itself proves, the company is notoriously litigious, or at least it was until this catastrophic legal own-goal. Secondly, McDonald's global advertising and marketing budget is colossal (US$1,800m in 1995), and media that are financed even partly by advertising risk the company's wrath at their peril. It is alleged, for example, that when the *Independent* carried a front-page story about McDonald's secret attempts to negotiate a settlement after only six weeks of the case, the company withdrew over US$120,000 of advertising from the *Independent on*

Still from 'Two Worlds Collide' – Credit: One-Off Productions

Sunday. In 1989, Channel 4 was forced to apologise in court and pay McDonald's costs after showing *Jungleburger*, in which the sales director of one of McDonald's' Costa Rican suppliers appeared to admit that beef he supplied to the company had been farmed on ranches created by deforestation.

But mystery surrounds another McDonald's film which was supposed to be shown on the channel but was never transmitted, *One Every Mile*. A persistent suggestion, however, is that C4 felt the filmmaker had been pushed into ceding too much editorial control to McDonald's.

Both these films are briefly quoted in Dennis Woolf's exemplary dramatisation of highlights of the trial, the three hour-plus *McLibel*, shown on C4 just before the verdict was announced. But even this has now run into problems, since the channel is refusing to sell it to overseas buyers unless they indemnify it against possible libel action by McDonald's. Apparently at least one foreign sale has thus been lost.

All this is as nothing, however, compared to the problems faced by *McLibel: Two Worlds Collide*, although only the *Guardian* has seen fit to cover them. Franny Armstrong set up her company, One-Off Productions, specifically to make this film and was among a number of independent producers who tried during the trial to interest the broadcasters in it. ITV told her there was 'not enough action'; the BBC didn't feel 'sufficiently enthusiastic'; and Channel 4 decided to put its resources behind Dennis Woolf.

Nothing daunted, Armstrong carried on filming. She wrote to McDonald's witnesses, asking to interview them, but the refusal letters came from the company's press office. So she persuaded Ken Loach to direct dramatised reconstructions of some of their courtroom evidence. She also interested Jane Balfour Films in the idea of distributing the film worldwide. Then, with media interest finally growing as the trial neared its climax, Armstrong struck lucky with the BBC's *Heart of the Matter* and, although no written contract was signed, the film was scheduled for 30 June 1997. The series editor, Anne Reevell, was clearly aware that the film posed certain problems: 60 minutes had to be reduced to 40; Helen Steel and Dave Morris' clandestine recording of McDonald's abortive settlement attempt almost certainly infringed BBC guidelines; the use of McDonald's advertisements raised copyright issues; and, last but not least, there was the question of libel. However, neither the BBC's lawyers nor Alan Yentob seemed to think the problems intractable, and Armstrong and Reevell worked together to try, in the latter's words, 'To turn the film into something the BBC could transmit.' In the end, however, she had to admit that 'it proved impossible to broadcast'. According to Armstrong, 'She kept having to send reports to Yentob and await his replies, it was all dragging out, the verdict was getting nearer and nearer and, when it was only 10 days away, Anne felt that she just couldn't go on with it.'

When the trial finished, there was a brief but unproductive flurry of interest from Channel 5 and *World in Action*; then, two months later, Armstrong met Alan Hayling, commissioning editor for documentaries at Channel 4, at the Sheffield Documentary Festival, and interested him in seeing the film. Hayling says he thought it 'a strong piece of work for a first-time film-maker, and I wanted to be able to do something with it'. But he adds, 'Right away I could see there were clear legal difficulties. The secretly recorded conversation with McDonald's lawyers was an obvious problem, but there was also the question of libel. Anyway I showed it to our legal department and their decision was very clear: nothing resembling this programme could be broadcast in Britain because it was repeating allegations that had already been found to be defamatory in the High Court. If we showed it, McDonald's was highly likely to sue us and win. Under such circumstances nobody would insure the programme against libel, and every C4 programme has to be insured against that'. Dennis Woolf got round this problem by sticking rigidly to quoting verbatim courtroom testimony, but what appears to have swayed Channel 4's lawyers (more than the BBC's) is that certain allegations found libellous by the trial judge are repeated outside the courtroom context by some of the participants in the programme. What Armstrong calls Channel 4's 'absolute categorical no' then put the wind up Jane Balfour, who regretfully decided that she couldn't sell *Two Worlds Collide* abroad in case foreign TV showings led to her being prosecuted by McDonald's under English libel law.

According to One-Off's legal adviser, Robin Lewis of Bindmans, 'Franny has produced a film in which she has reduced the libel risk to the minimum that is compatible with the kind of programme she wanted to produce. But when you're trying to assess libel risk you have to take into account not only the wording of an item but also if it is about the sort of person or organisation likely to sue for libel.' On the first point, Lewis feels 'the broadcasters seem to be arguing for a total elimination of all libel risk as opposed to eliminating the irreducible minimum compatible with a programme communicating what actually took place.' On the second, he says, 'One has the distinct feeling that if the programme were not about McDonald's but Joe's Café, the broadcasters' editorial courage might return.' However, he also believes that the company is less litigation-prone given the consequences of its 'barely rational' decision to sue Steel and Morris. On the other hand, as long as broadcasters continue to show themselves to be intimidated by McDonald's fearsome past record, the company has little to fear. Meanwhile, it's just the audience, hungry for knowledge about a company whose global activities raise some of the most important issues of our time, that's the loser. ❑

Julian Petley writes regularly for Index on film and video. He is a lecturer in Media and Communication Studies at Brunel University

The video of McLibel: Two Worlds Collide (£14.99) *is available from One-Off Productions, BCM Oops, London WC1N 3XX. It can also be viewed at www.spanner.org/mclibel/vdo. A feast of McLibel-related information also awaits at www.mcspotlight.org, which has to date received over 40 million visitors.*

PAUL O'CONNOR

'You have the right to remain silent...'

In Britain, reporting the news the mainstream media ignores is fast becoming a ticket to the cells

Dressed in a white paper suit and little else, documentary maker Ben Edwards blinked as the early sun rose over the police station in Plymouth. It was the end of his 24-hour stint in a small cell; his video camera and tapes were now in the hands of the police. Just another statistic in the growing number of journalists in Britain arrested in the line of duty.

For three months, Edwards had been documenting the direct-action protests against the test sites of genetically modified crops (GM) up and down the country. Activists have destroyed over two thirds of all GM test crops growing in the open air. Edwards had been given exclusive access by the activists to report their actions as they trashed a GM site near Totnes in Devon on 3 August. However, the police were tipped off and duly arrested all the activists, along with Edwards, despite his credentials as a journalist. While he was locked up, police raided his home and seized his computer, a number of video tapes and written material. Later, surrounded by the devastation of his home, Edwards said: 'They seem to have no idea what they were looking for, they even took tapes of documentaries I taped off the TV.' Despite the home raid, detention and confiscation of his clothes, the police have yet to charge him. He is due to appear back at Plymouth police station on 24 September.

The background to the police action is the increasingly heated debate on the safety of GM food. In August, it was revealed that the House Of Commons catering committee had banned genetically modified foods from the parliamentary canteen six months earlier, at a time when

Parliament itself was busy rejecting compulsory labelling of GM products for the benefit of consumers.

Even as Edwards sat in his cell it was reported that US researchers had witnessed supposedly sterile GM plants interbreeding with their natural cousins, exploding one of the key arguments supporting the release of GM test crops – that they are not capable of 'proliferation'. Yet the UK ministry of agriculture still staunchly supports the industry line, agreeing with Monsanto – a major developer of GM plants now spending US$1.5 million on a PR campaign in the UK– that the world of the next century will starve without GM food.

The police crackdown on news gathering goes beyond stifling GM protests. A few weeks prior to the Devon arrests, a journalist reporting for the *Daily Mail* was arrested in Ayrshire merely for knocking on a door. He was enquiring about a secret meeting of hugely influential capitalists known as the Bilderberg Group. A journalist for eight years, Campbell Thomas, 34, is also a special constable and his initial disbelief at his arrest for breach of the peace was followed by five hours in a filthy cell. Thomas said that 'it seems that the arresting of journalists has been going on for a long time but newspaper and TV editors rely so much on the police for tip-offs that they don't want to risk upsetting their prime source of news'. Despite all charges being dropped in court, he was suspended as a special constable.

Television reporter Roddy Mansfield came up against the Metropolitan Police while filming a protest against Rank Leisure Ltd. He showed his NUJ press card but couldn't remember the card's PIN. Mansfield was arrested for forging a press card. All charges were later dropped. However, he missed his deadline and the story ended up on the edit-suite floor. Since that incident, he feels he has been singled out for harassment by the police: he has been assaulted by riot police, had his camera smashed, been arrested six times and, in May this year, the Met erased all his camera footage in front of him in the custody suite of Belgravia police station. What they hadn't reckoned on was that his camera would pick up shots of their own feet and record their voices as they questioned him about him being a journalist. Mansfield sees it as his 'first real hard piece of evidence of police news management'.

Photographer Nick Cobbing was one of the few journalists convicted and fined for obstructing a bailiff despite the courts recognising him as a working reporter. He was arrested during the Manchester airport protests while working in the trees. While other journalists were corralled into the police-controlled pen, well away from the evictions, Cobbing managed to get into the trees where the news was actually happening. Cobbing is convinced the police have a covert plan: 'Since the police come under a lot of criticism for their policing methods, they want to put journalists off going to these events. The easiest to deter are the freelances because they don't have the backing of the large news organisation.' Another casualty at Manchester was HTV producer John Williams who was truncheoned over the head and dragged away from the protest site.

More worrying is the case of video journalist Gerard O'Sullivan who was arrested in April while reporting at a vivisection protest in Oxfordshire. He has the dubious honour of becoming the first journalist to be charged under the Protection from Harassment Act. Just who was being harassed by his filming remains open to debate but O'Sullivan has his suspicions: 'All I was doing was filming Thames Valley police handling a female protester roughly when officers suddenly yanked the camera from me and arrested me under this law.' Witney magistrates court will hear O'Sullivans case on 25 August. Sally Gilbert, lawyer for the National Union of Journalists (NUJ), says: 'This law was intended mainly to protect women who were being stalked. When it was passed in 1997 the NUJ warned that it would be used against journalists.'

It seems that the NUJ press card is no longer valid in the eyes of the police despite having been introduced by them. Association of Chief Police Officers (ACPO) spokesman Tim Mahoney denied the notion of police news management: 'Do the police set out to control and manipulate the media? No, there is no intent to do that.'

In the early part of this century press baron Lord Northcliffe defined the news as 'something someone, somewhere, wants to suppress; everything else is just advertising'. With the corporate take-over of the media it is all the more important that the real issues are reported and that journalists don't find themselves wandering the streets in white paper suits. ❏

Paul O'Connor is the producer of undercurrents *alternative news video. Subscription details page 195*

TATYANA TOLSTOYA

Colors of confusion

East is east and west is west, as *Colors* magazine found out when it launched its Russian-language version. Readers were baffled and the translators have much to answer for

It was the Italians who came up with the saying *traduttore-traditore* (the translator is a traitor). Not trusting translators overmuch, perhaps, in the Russian edition of Benetton's magazine *Colors*, the publishers have provided a parallel text in the world's *lingua franca*: English. Which is just as well, or we'd have understood nothing. There are plenty of worthless, 'yellow' magazines on Russian stalls, disporting themselves on all fours in front of the reader – 'come, buy me, I'm every bit as bad as you' – but at least their language corresponds to their content. *Colors* is a good journal and we have grown tired waiting for an original, quality magazine to appear. So we've got it. An incompetent team of ignoramuses has taken on a trifling job – the translation of a simple English text – and not only failed in something a child could have done better, but lost sight of the whole point of the magazine in the process.

In the first Russian issue of *Colors* we are given no indication of what kind of publication this is: a photographic journal – look and see for yourself. Here and there you get a cultural clue which requires no explanation in the European context, but remains hieroglyphics to a Russian reader. The cover calls it a 'magazine about the rest of the world'; a phrase which a European will instantly – and correctly – understand, but we won't. To a European – an adequately fed and reasonably civilised member of the middle class – 'the rest of the world' is the 'third' world: Asia, Africa, South America, with refugees, war and camps for the displaced. For Russians 'the rest of the world' indicates everything except ourselves, from Luxembourg to Mongolia. What's Asia to us? We are Asia. What are refugees to us? We have plenty of our own. What's hunger in Africa to us? We don't get our wages paid either. So *Colors*, sadly, is intended not for us but for the comfortably off who need to have their conscience pricked. Admittedly, there are adequately fed people in Russia too, but here conscience reclines in Morpheus's embrace.

Tatyana Tolstoya – Credit: Virago

The issue opens with the photograph of a family. A Polish family. Barely distinguishable from an average Muscovite family, or a family from Bibirovo or Cheremushki: cheerless curtains, tasteless bric-a-brac, everything spotless, lots of children round the table, and man's best friend – the telly – in pride of place. Faces with no spark of genius. Just like it is here. And this is a family from the Kingdom of Tonga. Where's that? Don't you know? Well, neither do we actually. But people live there too all the same: a barefoot granny sits on the floor, legs crossed, and fans herself with a palm leaf. The head of the family, likewise on the floor, in a garish shirt, has managed to roll up a green radish of terrifying proportions; a crowd of kids, hard to say whose, and lots of pictures (I'm tempted to say photographs) of Christ on the walls and bedside tables, little carpets with peacocks, flowers, garlands and little vases, four TV sets and two cassette recorders. They're living pretty well, though it's all a bit unfamiliar.

A St Petersburg communal flat, painfully recognisable, walls smeared with green oil-paint, nappies hung out to dry, pans overturned on the cooker, so the neighbours won't spit in them [a common petty crime in flats where many families share a communal kitchen]; pale faces.

The family of a Kenyan farmer. A complete *Vyshnii Volochok* of shabby provincialism, except that the faces are blacker than night and Dad has holes in his ear lobes big enough to put a log through. Some tribes insert huge round objects in their ears; vanity I think. It looks ridiculous, but don't we look ridiculous in our clothes, with our jewellery?

And having reminded you graphically, dear reader, that there are people just like you living the world over – giving birth, buying up junk, dreaming – the magazine goes on to what we once called 'howling' contrasts, which is exactly what they are. Human beings are all brothers (sisters, nephews, cousins, step-daughters and so on – it's the metaphor running through the issue), and while you fuss around in your clean little house (or flat), there, in the rest of the world, your brethren are having a bad time. And since humanity is one big family, what about a present or two for your dear ones then? And this is where text begins to appear on the page and the Russian translators, Katya and Seryozha, are onto it right away, like termites, chewing their way vigorously through a healthy tree of original writing and transforming it into a fat pile of meaningless sawdust.

The contrasts are as follows. In Romania, 3,000 children are down with AIDS, their parents have abandoned them, and the state has no money either to treat or support them. Meanwhile in Holland, an artist has constructed a folding, dual-use coffin for a child – cost US$2,500 – bright, cheerful, painted with sunflowers. While the child is still alive, the coffin can be used as a writing table or a book shelf. It looks like a narrow wardrobe with a desk. I think the designer is a monster. Wouldn't you like one for YOUR son?

Or there are those recently invented edible plates made of pressed starch, none too delicious, but ecologically sound: they disintegrate in the rubbish within two days. Is this not concern for the human race? Except that, ironically, 20 per cent of the world's population is hungry and has nothing to put on its plates – wooden, tin or a palm leaf. Go on, give an edible plate to YOUR sister!

In Congo there are 13,540 patients to every doctor and volunteers from Médecins sans Frontières are run off their feet helping the sick. In the USA they also care about people: a politically correct plaster of three different shades of brown has been devised for blacks of every complexion. Their sufferings will now be greatly alleviated. Wouldn't you like to give a plaster to YOUR family doctor?

The photos are accompanied by a short, neutral description: this is what people lack, and here is something to give as a gift. It's sold in the shops. Well? Work it out for yourself. The idea is that the absurd disparity between the 'presents' and people's real needs should shock. The intention is to inspire not pity, but anger; not to stand by waiting with an outstretched palm, but to plunge the reader face first into another's pain, while he struggles to evade it, blinker himself and hide. It's an effective ploy. In the African desert a boy tills the dry, infertile earth with his hoe. It's unlikely to yield anything: there's no water, and – don't hold your breath – there's none coming either. Why not send him those unusual earphones with sea shells, imitating the sound of the sea. He'll be able to listen to water then. And if you think this is some kind of a joke, then it's time you did something about it. When you next throw out an old pair of trousers, a stool or an old iron – stop! Dial a number, and people will come to take your rubbish and give it to someone who really needs it.

Such is the theme of the issue entitled:'Gifts'. Don't you want to do anything 'for those special people in your life' the magazine asks?

The Russian version reads: 'Surprise your family and friends.' Katya and Seryozha advise you not to be concerned about your neighbour, but to acquire something original to entertain you and the narrow circle of your rich friends. The 'coffin' with sunflowers, for your child, is in inverted commas, for instance. But this really is a coffin! The magazine is horrified that a Dutch designer has descended to such depths of moral kitsch while children are indeed dying. Katya and Seryozha are dancing on graves. Never mind the black humour and the post-modernism. 'If you get blown up by a land mine...' the magazine writes brutally – dozens of Nicaraguan children are blown up by mines daily. 'If, God forbid, you should be blown up...' K&S slip in coyly; to them, the suffering of some bunch of Nicaraguans is zilch.

In their translation, Niger becomes Nigeria, the Kingdom of Tonga the African state of Togo. The preoccupations of the editors of *Colors* is a matter of complete indifference to them. *Colors* says: 'Open your eyes, wake up! There are people out there, in distant countries, islands and deserts.' The translators yawn: sod them.

Sluggishly, with their sleeves rolled down, they doodle incoherently: 'When farmers weed land to achieve a good harvest, the results can be the reverse?' But is land weeded? And when did weeding lead to a poor harvest? The English says: 'When farmers clear land to grow crops...'

Or this: 'During cultivation, the top layer of soil breaks up into chemical elements...' You don't have to be an expert on soils to wince. The English text reads: 'As top soil becomes exposed to the elements the wind, the sun, droughts...' The message of this sad text is that when forests are cut down, the country becomes a desert. But what's that to us? So it happens; too bad.

They (or the computer?) translate 'glasses' as 'attention' (*vnimaniye*); 'records' as 'tape recorders' (*magnitofony*); 'this illness is difficult to treat' as 'this is difficult to interpret'. 'Education' becomes 'clothes'; 'blacksmiths' are 'skilled craftsmen'; 'entrance fee' becomes 'intoductory payment'; 'merchandising' is rendered as 'the commercial value of Leonardo's paintings' (?!). 'Carpets' become 'socks'; 'multiple sclerosis' 'sclerotic phenomena'; 'more' becomes 'less'; and the simple sentence 'a big dog can be overpowering for a frail owner' is rendered as 'the large beast has a negative effect on the psyche of his sickly master'.

In the Philippines it is very, very humid. In the rainy season children in orphanages can't get their clothes to dry. The magazine invites its readers to send them their old drying machines. K&S transform them into washing machines. They can't imagine that in a huge, indifferent world (why not in Russia too?) there could be just one kind soul who might take pity on these Filipino orphans and send them what they need. You can imagine the long faces of the orphans as they unpack their parcel in the downpour and there, like an insult, emerges a contraption that will make their wet underwear even wetter. There are monsters in Russia, their carers will think. In the entire 86 pages of the journal there isn't one where the text isn't so thoroughly and repeatedly misinterpreted that it becomes a complete travesty of the original. And if the translators don't understand what something is about, they simply ignore it.

On the back cover there is a photograph of a fat family: spherical Mum and Dad and two incurably piggy little girls. The translation reads 'Family during a "Cruise to Lose", Miami, USA.' So what? the Russian reader asks. The idea is that, having closed the journal, the thoughtful reader, a decent person, a good Samaritan, will be especially stung by this strategically placed photograph. 'Cruise to Lose' is an expensive US sea trip for super-gluttons: the sort with oil spurting out of their pores when you touch them; for those who eat with four spoons all at once, denying themselves nothing, for big money. And when they have keeled over and found they're up to their ears in lard, spend more big money to shake off a few kilo. If they want to explain this to a Russian reader, it might be a good idea if the translators understood it; and that's just what they refuse to do. They seem to be on indefinite intellectual strike.

But the zenith of their achievement must be the transfiguration of the heading 'Wooden penis' into 'Wooden's penis'. These wooden models are produced in South Africa 'not for internal use', but to provide training in the use of condoms, should you happen to need it. The manufacturer calls them 'Wooden Willies'. Predictably, in their unequal battle on two fronts – with syntax and meaning – K&S have muddled their parts of speech in English, as much as their South African body-parts, and transformed the obscure producer of these phalluses into the 'entrepreneur' Willie Wooden.

It's a useful little nick-knack and, at US$5.15, inexpensive too. So why don't the publishers of *Colors* follow the example of Russian entrepreneurs and pay the translators in Willies for their pains? ❏

Tatyana Tolstaya *is a writer and journalist. She works in Russia and the USA, writing for several Russian newspapers and also teaching at Skidmore College. Translated by Irena Maryniak*

Cruising to war

Sometime in 1993, a friend told me an odd little tale. The courtyard of Islamabad's Faisal Mosque – kindly donated to Pakistan at the cost of many million dollars by Saudi Arabia – had suddenly erupted with hosts of bearded and turbaned young men from all corners of the globe – Africans, Arabs, Central Asians as well as Pakistanis. Every morning, he said, they were drilled in unarmed combat by a black instructor he discovered was from Atlanta, Georgia. He observed them every day for a few months until, as suddenly as they had appeared, they vanished. Six months later, the taliban erupted into Afghanistan and onto the world stage.

As we go to press, the world's 'flashpoints' have just one thing in common: the spark that ignited them springs from Washington. Not only Nairobi, Dar es-Salaam, Khartoum and Kabul, but Albania, where the present drama began when 200 US marines landed in the capital, Tirana, to pull out the entire US diplomatic staff just a week before the missiles flew; Pakistan, most loyal vassal of the USA, where mobs are now burning the Stars and Stripes and threatening the survival of the government; and, once again, Baghdad, where Saddam Hussein will draw maximum benefit from imperial America's latest adventure in the Muslim world.

Forget the timing: every commentator in the region knews it was coming sooner or later. They've all seen *Wag the Dog*; they know the score. Nor is it the first time a US president has started a small war to save his political skin back home. And it worked. A press corps that had been snapping at the presidential heels with increasing ferocity, keeled over and appears to be doing its utmost to assist the administration in preparing US public opinion for 'a prolonged battle' in what Secretary of State Madeleine Albright calls 'the war of the future'.

So much for the fourth estate, the watchdog and guardian of the public interest. Despite the fact that no hard evidence of the 'imminent terrorist threat to US interests' has been produced; that other, reliable sources say the pharmaceutical factory in Khartoum was no more than it claims; that Osama bin Laden, the man Washington now demonises with an insistence matched only by that applied to another former ally, Saddam Hussein, was well known to the CIA long before CNN introduced this so-called 'shadowy' figure into US homes; or that they have yet to produce proof of his connection to the attacks in Kenya and Tanzania more convincing than 'confessions' planted in the Pakistani press, to a network the US media is prepared to play the President's game.

Most disturbing is that they appear to be willing to do so in a state of complete ignorance and blind faith. Speaking on US television, Senator John McCain, told his interviewer, 'Our problem is that we are in the habit of giving you too much information. More often than not, that serves to inform the enemy.' As General Hugh Shelton, who refused to answer journalists' questions at the first Pentagon press briefing after the missile attacks, confirmed, things were going to be different this time. 'During Desert Storm [against Iraq], we briefed you fully after each operation. This time we're playing a different game: our business is with terrorists.'

So with no state nor organisation in the world to challenge it, and its media in thrall,the USA will risk world peace behind a wall of secrecy and the public will be none the wiser

For the last two decades, the USA has played with fire in the Muslim world: it has stacked, stoked and fuelled the conflagrations that now threaten it with the mischievous and inconsequent abandon of a small boy with an oversize box of matches. From its US$2 billion backing of an Islamic *mujahedin* to drive the Soviet army from Afghanistan, to the creation of the super monster in the shape of the taliban to sort out the post-Soviet internecine squabbles of the same *mujahedin*, to its use of bin Laden to further its aims in both cases, the USA has played Islamic radicals at both ends in pursuit of its own short-term ends. As in Iraq, the good guys and the bad are one and the same. 'Good' Islamic guerrillas make 'bad' Islamic terrorists when agendas part company. Washington first embraces and then demonises the creatures of its own making.

Now that its dogs have slipped the leash, and as befits its sole superpower status, their handler has shouldered the burden of reigning them in alone and unaided. It is, after all, their self-proclaimed mission to 'make the world safe for democracy'. In the meantime, the only tangible result they appear to have achieved is to radicalise Islamic sentiment throughout the Muslim world, cut the ground from under their 'moderate' allies in the region and spread bin Laden's fame and credibility to a degree he could not have dreamed of. There'll be little room for democracy, even less for for the rights of peoples and nations and none at all for 'truth', already among the casualties in this 'clash of civilisations' Clinton has succesfully shifted from the pages of an academic journal to the world stage.

The price for your salvation is too high, Mr President. ❏

JVH

A censorship chronicle incorporating information from the American Association for the Advancement of Science Human Rights Action Network (AAASHRAN), Amnesty International (AI), Article 19 (A19), the BBC Monitoring Service Summary of World Broadcasts (SWB), the Committee to Protect Journalists (CPJ), the Canadian Committee to Protect Journalists (CCPJ), the Inter-American Press Association (IAPA), the International Federation of Journalists (IFJ/FIP), the International Federation of Newspaper Publishers (FIEJ), Human Rights Watch (HRW), the Media Institute of Southern Africa (MISA), International PEN (PEN), Open Media Research Institute (OMRI), Radio Free Europe/Radio Liberty (RFE/RL), Reporters Sans Frontières (RSF), the World Association of Community Broadcasters (AMARC), the World Association of Newspapers (WAN), the World Organisation Against Torture (OMCT) and other sources

AFGHANISTAN

In late July the Taliban issued an edict by radio forbidding parents to give children such 'non-Muslim' names as Rita, Parkash and Guita, all of which had featured in the Indian films popular before the religious movement's rise to power. (SWB)

Recent Publication: *The Taliban's war on women: A health and human rights crisis in Afghanistan* (Physicians for Human Rights, August 1998)

ALGERIA

On 26 June the Berber singer **Lounés Matoub**, who only recently returned from exile in France, was gunned down at a bogus roadblock on the road to his village in Beni Douala. Matoub was outspoken in his opposition to both the government and the Islamist groups. On 1 July, the Armed Islamic Group claimed responsibility for the murder, calling Matoub 'among the most stubborn enemies of religion'. (*Guardian*, Reuters, *Middle East International*)

On 5 July thousands of Berbers took to the streets to reiterate a long-standing demand for official recognition of their Tamasheq language as the government began to enforce a new law providing for fines of up to 10,000 dinars ($ 170) for officials or business executives who sign any deal or statement not drafted in Arabic. Up to 5 million of the 30 million population are Berber-speakers. A statement sent to the newspapers *el-Watan* and *Le Matin* on 2 July announced the formation of the Armed Berber Movement (ABM), declaring that the movement would 'eliminate' those who 'try to apply the government's Arabisation policy'. The ABM also vowed to 'kill all those who contributed directly or indirectly to the killing of our spiritual leader Lounés Matoub.' Thousands of protesters marched through Algiers on 9 July in a protest organised by the Socialist Forces Front, a leading secular Berber opposition party. (Reuters, *Financial Times*)

The government has failed to keep promises on freedom of the press made in March 1998 by Communications Minister Habib-Chawki Hamraoui to a delegation from the World Association of Newspapers (*Index* 3/1998). No legal action against reporters has been lifted, and in May journalist Ihsan el-Khadi was detained as he was about to travel to an international conference and jailed for a year on defamation charges (*Index* 4/1998). Visa restrictions and 'security' controls on foreign journalists remain unchanged and foreign newspapers remain unavailable. (RSF)

Four journalists ended a three-week hunger strike on 23 July after receiving guarantees they would not be moved to a distant hotel where their safety could not be assured. The four began their fast on 2 July in protest against official plans to rehouse them and colleagues at the Matarès hotel in Tipaza province, an Islamist stronghold 70km from the capital. The journalists, all of whom work in Algiers, had been ordered to quit their emergency residences at the Mazafroun tourist complex, about 20km west of the city, but they refused, claiming the government had no plans to provide security. On 14 July, about 100 journalists protested in solidarity outside the Algiers offices of Prime Minister Ahmed Ouyahia. (*Guardian*, IFJ, Reuters)

ARGENTINA

Ex-dictator Jorge Rafael Videla was arrested on 9 June for

offering for adoption to families with links to the armed forces children born in captivity to kidnapped pregnant women. Videlha remained unpunished thanks to impunity laws which prevent the prosecution of military personnel for human rights violations, but the laws do not exclude the crime of 'appropriation of minors', with which the former head of state is being charged. On 13 July, federal judge **Roberto Marquevich**, who ordered the arrest, received an anonymous message saying 'we have decided to take justice in our own hands and condemn you to death from this moment'. (Derechos Humanos, AI, *Independent, El Pais*)

On 21 June the Italian government became the plaintiff in the trial of military officers involved in the disappearance of Italian nationals during the dictatorship from 1976-83. Accused are Juan Carlos Girardi, Julio Roberto Rossin, Alejandro Puertas, Jose Luis Porchetto and Omar Héctor Maldonado, all allegedly responsible for the death of eight Italian nationals. (Equipo Nizkor)

AZERBAIJAN

On 28 July presidential aide Ali Hasanov was reported as saying that the authorities will not allow any 'destabilising' measures during the run-up to the 11 October presidential elections. On 8 July, five opposition candidates from the Movement for Democratic Reforms and Democratic Elections (MDRDE) had announced plans to stage a mass rally in Baku on 15 August to protest against the law on the presidential elections which, according to a MDRDE spokesperson, allows President Haydar Aliyev to name all members of the Central Election Commission. Western diplomats in Baku agree that the law practically precludes the possibility of a free and fair election. (Reuters, RFE/RL)

BANGLADESH

It was reported on 22 July that the government had imposed an immediate ban on women seeking employment overseas as nurses and housemaids to 'protect them from abusive employers'. The move follows several cases of women abroad being subjected to sexual and other forms of abuse. Human rights organisations said the ban violates women's right to freedom of movement. (SWB)

On 26 July the foreign ministry issued an order denying journalists the right of entry to the ministry's premises without special permission. It also instructed its staff not to talk to journalists. The decisions followed articles in the local press about the Status of Forces Agreement, signed with the US government, and alleged pressure on the government to allocate exploration of an oil and gas field to a US company. (Media Watch

BELARUS

On 10 June it was announced that President Alyksandr Lukashenka will introduce new measures which would extend existing laws criminalising the defamation of public officials, to punish anybody deemed to have 'insulted the president publicly' with up to four years imprisonment. In a proposed amendment to another law, anybody carrying placards and banners, or disseminating information in the media which may 'degrade the honour and dignity of the president,' will face substantial fines. (A9)

In the continuing sewage saga at the Drazdy diplomatic complex (*Index* 4/1998), President Lukashenka accused western states on 25 June of having taken 'a household issue and turned it into an international problem'. Claiming 'deliberate' provocation, the president assured the Crans Montana conference in Switzerland the following day that his country was civilised, citing the flow of foreign investment from McDonald's and Coca-Cola as evidence. He was supported by Russian Communist party leader Gennadii Zyuganov, who said the dispute was an attempt to break up the Belarus-Russian union. However, the departing Bulgarian ambassador countered by labelling the state 'a complete anachronism...a piece of shrapnel where the Soviet idea survived'. Meanwhile, in a resolution adopted on 16 July, the EU Parliament backed a Council ban on visas for senior officials until Lukashenka fully restored use of the ambassadors' residences. (RFE/RL)

On 12 August the Supreme Economic Court was due to pass judgement on the destiny of the state's oldest newspaper, *Nasha Niva*. Founded in 1906, the socio-political weekly is the only independent paper to publish solely in the Belarusian language. The paper is threatened with closure after using a 'non-Soviet' Belarusian orthography, thereby contravening a decree of the Council of Peoples Commissars of the Socialist Republic in 1993. (*Nasha Niva*)

BELGIUM

In late July Flemish television listings magazine *Humo* printed an interview with a family after all its members were dead through violence. Ann and Bob Gooseens were shot by their parents' Leo and Erna, who then killed themselves. The family had been engaged in a property dispute. Leo had suggested in the interview that he was considering 'drastic action' and *Humo* heavily promoted the article and the issue in which it appeared. (*Guardian*)

BOSNIA-HERZEGOVINA

On 1 July a UN police spokesman said it had launched an investigation into charges that Bosnian Serb police were running an organised prostitution ring with women from eastern Europe and the former USSR. (RFE/RL)

BULGARIA

On 15 July the Constitutional Court ruled that articles 146, 147 and 148, which punish 'libel' and 'insult' against state authority, did not contradict the constitution and therefore did not have to be rescinded. Journalists can thus still be imprisoned for six months for 'libel', or insulting a state representative. (RSF)

On 29 July prosecutor Kety Bozukova blocked the bank account of the Sliven weekly regional newspaper *Sedmitza*. Bozukova demanded a fine of 1 million levas (US$600) after the paper published an article criticising her work. Recently *Sedmitza* was fined 10 million levas (US$6,000) for 'libelling' Eva Jetcheva, vice-president of the parliamentary ruling party. (RSF)

BURMA

On the eve of the 10th anniversary of the democracy movement riots, the military regime cracked down on the opposition in early July, detaining at least 40 members of the National League for Democracy (NLD) and forcing others to sign pledges which restrict their movements. Officials said the move was a precaution against the opposition's scheme to create 'confrontation and instability' and to prevent a 'head-on collision' with authorities when colleges and universities reopen. Diplomats in Rangoon claim that this move is a result of the NLD's call on parliament to reconvene by 21 August. (*Financial Times*)

Democratic opposition leader **Aung San Suu Kyi** was forcibly driven home on 29 July after a six day road-side stand-off with the military junta. Suu Kyi, suffering from dehydration and a fever, was otherwise unhurt except for bruising to her wrists. The NLD leader was stopped by police 40 miles outside the capital while on her way to a supporters' meeting. She had been prevented from reaching her destination on two previous occasions but, this time, refused to turn back until the junta agreed to release political prisoners and hold a political dialogue. Her requests were ignored and the Nobel Prize laureate spent six nights trapped in her car. (*The Times, Far East Economic Review, Independent, Financial Times*)

BURUNDI

On 8 July it was announced that six detainees had been extra-judicially executed during the previous two weeks. **Speciose Butore, Didace Bukoru, Jean Ndabagamye, Karidou Mugabonihera** and **Ancalet Bambara** are reported to have been executed on 1 July in a detention cell in Gitenga province. They were arrested around 26 June and accused of collaboration with armed groups. (AI)

CAMBODIA

On 17 June the government banned all demonstrations and political rallies in Phnom Penh before the 26 July general election in order to ensure 'stability and a neutral political atmosphere in the city'. On 21 June more than 2,500 supporters of oppositon leader Sam Rainsy held a public rally in the capital, defying the ban.

(Reuters, *International Herald Tribune, Far East Economic Review*)

On 24 June, the National Election Commission announced a further ban on the publication of any articles relating to political parties. A day later, the editors of seven newspapers declared that the government's order was in breach of freedom of expression and they would ignore it. They called upon the international community to support their cause. (*Herald Sun*)

CAMEROON

At the end of June it was reported that imprisoned editor and journalist **Puis Njawe** (*Index* 3/1998, 4/1998) was suffering from an eye ailment for which prison authorities had refused to allow proper medical treatment. (WAN)

On 2 July **Patrick Tchouwa**, director of publication at the private magazine *Le Jeune Détective*, was arrested by police at a hotel in Yaoundé. The journalist's arrest is most likely because of an article published on 25 June which linked the Minister of Economy and Finance and a deputy to the embezzlement of public funds. (RSF)

CANADA

Fairview Technology Centre Ltd, a British Columbia-based internet service provider, ceased operations on 26 May under pressure from a telephone company upset about the firm's links with

European white-power groups. Fairview hosted web pages for the French Charlemagne Hammer Skinheads, which contained death threats against Jews and European human-rights activists. Owner **Bernard Klatt** said the Hammer Skins' contract with him ended in March, after 13 members of the group were jailed by French police, and that he had no contact with them since then. Fairview is still under investigation by the province's attorney-general. (Reuters)

A journalist for CFRN News in Edmonton, Alberta, has been notified that she was the object of surveillance between 27 January and 28 March this year. **Janice Johnston** received the letter in early June from Chief Crown Prosecutor Gary McQuaig, but it did not tell her who conducted the surveillance, how it was done, or what communications were intercepted. Johnston produced a story in 1997 about an internal investigation into the alleged criminal connections of a member of the Edmonton police. While the interception of private communications may be authorised by a judge, Johnston has no legal right to view the documents or to know why the order was approved: the law simply dictates that the subject must be informed after a communication has been intercepted. This appears to be the first known instance of a journalist having private communications intercepted. (CCPJ)

British physicist **Laurence**

Godfrey, who launched the UK's first internet libel case five years ago after he was abused for calling Canada 'boring', won a settlement in late June from an Australian internet service provider. Now Godfrey is prepared to go to Britain's High Court over Cornell student Michael Dolenga's remarks about him, but no-one is sure which libel laws apply: those of the UK, Canada or the US, where the libel was committed. (*Financial Times*)

Thirteen years after the world's sixth-worst air disaster, police are keeping secret reports into the explosion that killed 329 Air India passengers over the Irish coast. Although investigators believe there was a bomb, they refuse to say what evidence has been found, or when the reports will be released. The Royal Canadian Mounted Police said it wanted to maintain secrecy in order to preserve its chances of prosecution. (Reuters)

Recent Publications: *Limited Access: Assessing the health of Canada's freedom of information laws* (Queen's University Press), July 1998.

CHINA

In response to the launching of the Chinese version of the online Catholic news service Fides on 4 June, the government warned the Vatican not to use the Internet or other media channels to interfere with its religious affairs policies. (Electronic Frontier Foundation)

Four dissidents were reported to have been detained on President Clinton's arrival in Xi'an on 25 June. The Information Center of Human Rights and Democratic Movement in China claimed on 28 June that **Yang Hai** and human rights lawyer **Zhang Jiankang** were released as Clinton left the city. However, dissident **Li Xiaolong** was still being held while **Zhou Jianhe** was made to leave the city ahead of Clinton's arrival. (Reuters)

The Broadcasting Authority in Hong Kong fined a local television network HK$13,000 for broadcasting an interview with a reputed Macau gang leader. The Authority believed that the discussion on how 'Broken Tooth' Koi had acquired his wealth and gambling habits would be a 'bad influence' on the listeners. (*Far East Economic Review*)

Former editor of the *Oriental Daily News* **Wong Yeung-ng** was sentenced to four months for contempt of court on 30 June and the paper was fined HK$1.08 million. The paper had been unhappy with a ruling in December 1997 which had prevented it from taking *Apple Daily* to court for reproducing pictures. Following the court decision the *Oriental Daily News* ran a series of articles calling the judiciary 'white pigs' and 'scumbags.' SAR legislator Emily Lau Wai-hing said: 'I don't think journalists would see this as a big threat.' (*Far East Economic Review, South China Morning Post, Straits Times*)

Zhu Yufu, a pro-democracy activist based in Hangzhou, was detained on 30 June for issuing a manifeso of the Chinese Democratic Party, the first opposition party to be formed. **Wang Youcai**, one of the party's founding dissidents, had tried unsuccessfully to register the party on 25 June and was also detained, along with 11 others. Wang Youcai and Lin Hui remain in detention facing charges of 'harming state security'. (Reuters)

The Hong Kong Journalists Association on 28 June released its annual report 'Questionable Beginnings' which warned of a gradual erosion of the freedom of the press. The association's chairman, Carol Lai, said that the government had become less transparent and the trend on self-censorship in particular to national security issues was worrying. (SWB)

Cameras were allowed into the Beijing first intermediate people's court to give the first live television broadcast of a trial on 9 July. Xiao Yang, president of the supreme people's court, called it an initiative to replace 'darkroom trials' with open trials. (*Financial Times*)

The leader of a hacking group, who is known as Blondie Wong, formed on 14 July a new global hacking organisation, the Yellow Pages, to protest western investment in China. (Derechos Humanos)

Zhang Shanguang, a dissident trying to form a pressure group for redundant workers, was detained on 22

July. He was taken from his home in Xupu. He had served seven years for his participation in the 1989 democracy movement. (Reuters)

Recent Publications: *Human rights one year on: No room for complacency* (AI, June 1988); *Detention and harassment of dissidents and others between January and June 1998* (AI, June 1998); *Nine years after Tiananmen. Ssill a counter-revolutionary riot?* (AI, June 1998)

On 24 May soldiers slaughtered a stolen cow, telling the numerous witnesses they would use the same 'technique' to kill **Eduard**, an ordained member of the human rights organisation Peace and Justice. Army officials went to Eduard's residence on 17 June, forcing him to name and give details about witnesses to the incident. (Equipo Nizkor)

On 18 June a home-made bomb exploded at the offices of Zagreb-based independent weekly *Imperial*. Nobody was injured, although the explosion caused extensive material damage. (RSF)

Several foreign news correspondents were thrown out of the National Assembly on 21 July so that President Fidel Castro might 'speak with complete freedom'. The journalists were reporting the opening of a new congressional session. (Inter American Press Association)

DEMOCRATIC REPUBLIC OF CONGO

The newly appointed director of national television was arrested in early June, only a fortnight after taking up his post.. He has reportedly been accused of 'sabotage and negligence', and for omitting to broadcast a government ceremony. His predecessor was also arrested for broadcasting shots of alleged massacre sites. (IRIN)

The state news agency ACP reported on 26 June that President Laurent Kabila has ordered the release of five journalists. The order followed a local press meeting in Kinshasa during which editors and journalists invited the president to guarantee freedom of expression. (IRIN)

On 30 June a UN human-rights team report stated that military forces of President Laurent Kabila massacred Rwandan Hutu refugees in 1996 and 1997. It called for an international tribunal to prosecute individuals within the ruling Alliance of Democratic Forces for the Liberation of the Congo and elements of the Rwandan army. The team, which had a mandate to investigate violations of international humanitarian law, was withdrawn in April because of the government's 'total lack of cooperation'. (*Washington Post*, IRIN)

DOMINICAN REPUBLIC

Law student **Franklin Bartolo Fabian** was shot dead on 6 July when police using guns and tear gas broke up a students' protest at the Autonomous University of Santo Domingo. The Dominican Students Federation (DFS) had called students to protest against a new rule mandating expulsion of students with bad grades, rule that the federation claims is illegal. (*El Diario, La Prensa*)

EAST TIMOR

A protestor was killed in front of visiting EU officials during a pro-independence demonstration on 8 July outside St. Antonio Cathedral. Angered by the officials carrying arms into the cathedral grounds, the 5,000-strong crowd mobbed the van carrying the diplomats and pelted it with stones. (*Far East Economic Review*)

EGYPT

Muhammad 'Abd al-Mun'im, the newly appointed editor of state-owned *Rose al-Yousef* (*Index* 4/1998), dismissed 15 'trainee' journalists on 1 June. Some had worked for the newspaper for five years, but reclassification as trainees is a tactic frequently used by state-owned publications to justify dismissing experienced journalists, or to keep them from joining the press syndicate. (*Cairo Times*)

Magdi Ahmad Hussein, editor-in-chief of the opposition newspaper *al-Sha'ab*, and the journalist **Mohammed Hilal**, were released on 3 July, one day after their jail sentences were overturned by the Court of Cassation. The court found procedural irregularities in their original convictions for libelling Alaa al-Alfi, son of former Interior Minister Hasan al-Alfi, in a 1996 series of articles accusing him of corruption. The two men became the first Egyptians jailed for criminal libel on 24 February (*Index* 6/1997, 2/1998, 3/1998). (Egyptian Organisation for Human Rights, *Cairo Times*, AI)

Freelance journalist **'Abd al-Mun'im Gamal al-Din** was reported on 8 July to have called off the hunger strike he began on 10 May (*Index* 4/1998) and to have been transferred to Tora Prison hospital for treatment. 'Abd al-Mun'im was protesting at his continued illegal detention since 21 February, despite being acquitted by a military court in October of involvement with an Islamic militant group. (AI)

Recent publications: *Empty stomachs and polluted water— Conditions in Abu Zaabal prisons* (EOHR, April 1998, 26pp); *The Belqas tragedy—Torture in Egypt's police stations* (EOHR, May 1998, 18pp)

EL SALVADOR

Trade union leader **Vicente Ramirez** was released on 16 June after being illegally detained on 25 May. The detention of Ramirez who is the Deputy Secretary-General of the Autonomous Centre of the Salvadoran Workers and president of the National Association of Workers, Sellers and Small Businessmen is thought to be related to his opposition to the eviction of 300 families working in the Mercado de Mayoreo de la Tiendona. (The Observatory, The Human Rights Actions Network)

ERITREA

Correction: In *Index* 4/1998 it was reported that **Ruth Simon** of AFP had been arrested on 25 April 1998. She was in fact arrested on 25 April a year earlier but still remains in prison. (RSF)

ETHIOPIA

On 8 July, the publisher and editor of the weekly *Genanaw*, **Zegeye Haile**, was fined US$1,430 and given a two-year suspended sentence for publishing 'libellous' articles. The government will enforce the suspended sentence should Zegeye publish any story considered offensive by the government over the next four years.(NDIMA)

On 13 July **Shimelis Kamal**, **Berhane Negash** and **Teferi Mekonnen**, all of *Nishan* newspaper, were arrested in Addis Ababa. Their arrests follow an article published in *Nishan* warning against ethnic animosity and criticising the government's detention and deportation of Eritreans. The journalists were released a day later and then rearrested after issuing a statement criticising their arrests. (IFJ, AI)

EUROPEAN UNION

On 1 July, the European Commission recommended that member states ban rubber ducks and other PVC toys. There may be a link between the ingestion of phthalate chemicals by children and cancer in later life. An outright ban, favoured by consumer affairs commissioner Emma Bonino, was avoided on political grounds. Bonino has also introduced a 'euro-label' for display in shop windows throughout the Union. The hallmark will be available to those outlets which pass on publicity material regarding the single currency to their customers. Those who actually accept the euro in transactions will receive a top grade label. Outlets are also being encouraged to display dual pricing on items and at tills. (*European, Guardian*)

On 30 July **Kristina Sheffield** and **Rachel Horsham** lost their fight to be legally recognised as females by the British authorities. Of the 40 signatories to the European Convention on Human Rights, only 4, including Britain, forbid transsexuals to change their passports and marry their chosen partners. The European Court in Strasbourg narrowly ruled against them. (*Guardian*)

FIJI

On 3 July a High Court judge in Suva quashed an application for an injunction by a major local retailer to stop details of the sale of the company being reported in the press. The judge deemed the injunction

an 'unwarranted cutailment' of the right to freedom of expression of the news and business magazine *Review*. Burns Phelp (Fiji) Limited claimed details of its possible sale reported in the June issue were defamatory. (PINA)

The Emergency Powers Act passed by the House of Representatives on 10 July enables the 'censorship and the control of and suppression of publications, writings, maps, plans, photographs, communications and means of communications'. The Act is a manifestation of the power of the president to declare a state of emergency on the advice of the government. (PINA)

FRANCE

In late July, an election result in Toulon which saw the National Front lose its only parliamentary seat was reversed. Television show host Karl Zero made comments which could have been construed as party propaganda on the same day as the poll thereby contravening electoral rules. The constitutional council therefore annulled the result. (*Guardian*)

Former British intelligence service operatives **David Shayler** and **Richard Tomlinson** were seized by police in Paris on 1 August, after they had threatened to publicise sensitive information. (*The Sunday Times*)

GERMANY

In late July the Bundesbank and state archive in Koblenz issued a report stating that documents detailing the property stolen from Holocaust victims had been 'mislaid'. Jewish activists, who did not accept the official explanation that the loss of the files was purely accidental, demanded an official investigation. (*Guardian, International Herald Tribune*)

GHANA

On 23 July the court of appeal found **Haruna Atta**, editor of the *Weekend Statesman*, and **Kweku Baako** of the *Guide*, guilty of contempt of court and sentenced them to one month's imprisonment. Their publishers, Kinesic Publications and Western publications respectively, were fined US$3,000. The two journalists were found guilty of publishing libellous material about first lady Nana Konadu Rawlings, thereby contravening an earlier court order preventing them from doing so. The two have since been moved from the Nsawam Prison near Accra to jails further away from the capital which are renowned for their poor conditions. (Free Expression Ghana)

Ebenezer Ato Sam, suspended editor of the *Free Press*, was found guilty of contempt of court on 27 July and sentenced to 21 days in prison, after defaulting on a US$2,000 fine. The conviction arose after a libel charge was brought by Local Government Minister Kwamena Ahwoi, who had been accused of siphoning ministry funds to finance his brother's cocoa business. The minister was awarded costs of US$870. (Free Expression Ghana)

GUATEMALA

On 20 July priest **Sebastiano Crestani** from the San Carlos de Borroneo church was the target of a gun attack, receiving wounds to his head, stomach and legs. Although he survived the attack he is still seriously ill in hospital. Crestani combines his spiritual duties with lecturing and journalism. (Equipo Nizkor)

HUNGARY

On 2 July entrepreneur **Jozsef Tamas Boros** and three pedestrians were killed by a bomb in the downtown tourist area of Budapest. Twenty-five other people were injured in the attack, which is thought to have been directed at Boros after he provided information to police investigating organised crime and the illegal oil trade. Three attempts had been made on his life in the previous two years and his home was under police protection. (RFE/RL)

INDIA

On 7 July **Mathew Marak**, editor of the daily *Achik Mikasal*, received a letter containing death threats from rebels belonging to the separatist Achik National Volunteer Council. The guerillas said in their letter that Marak had written several reports which were 'not correct'. (RSF)

Three of **Maqbool Fida Hussain**'s paintings are again being investigated for insulting Hinduism because they depict the goddesses Saraswati, Draupadi, and Sita in the nude (*Index* 3/1998). In early July the federal government, dominated by the Hindu-chauvinist Bharatiya Janata Party, gave permission to Delhi police to go ahead with a complaint made against Hussain by a member of the Vishwa Hindu Parishad (World Hindu Congress). Hussain, who has apologised for any offence his paintings may have caused, recently had his home in Bombay attacked by Hindu militants. (SWB)

In early July a court issued arrest warrants against media boss **Rupert Murdoch** for refusing to answer charges that his Star TV network had shown obscene films. The magistrate said three summons had been sent to Murdoch in the US and Australia but he had refused to accept them. It is alleged that films shown by his network, such as *Big Bad Mama* and *Stripped to Kill*, could 'damage the country's social fabric'. (SWB)

On 12 July **Puyam Theiba**, a reporter for the newspaper *Panthungfam*, was assaulted and injured by soldiers in the north-eastern state of Manipur when they raided his house. The soldiers claimed the journalist was involved in anti-Indian activities. **Arup Kumar Sarma**, editor of the magazine *Chitranjalee*, was also reportedly assaulted on 17 July by soldiers at Nalbari in the state of Assam. Assaults on journalists in the north-east are allegedly on the increase. (RSF)

On 18 July the government of Maharashtra decided to stop

the Mumbai (Bombay) performance of a play dealing with independence leader Mahatma Gandhi. The play - *Mee Nathuram Godse Boltoy*, or *I Nathuram Godse, Speaking'* - focuses on the Hindu nationalist Nathuram Godse, who opposed Gandhi's liberal views on minorities,and later assassinated him on 30 January 1948. State law makers claim the play depicts Gandhi as 'soft and helpless'. (Reuters)

INDONESIA

On 9 June, **Bob Hassan**, the timber-baron owner of the *Paron*, arbitrarily shut down his weekly paper citing poor sales. But the closure took place after the circulation had reportedly increased from 30,000 to 70,000. One report suggested the real reason was a series of investigative features on former president Suharto's wealth, which included titles such as 'Suharto's Family's Land as Big as Jakarta'. (*Far East Economic Review*)

In a decree dated 2 July, President Habibie stated that foreigners are still barred from investing in the local media. (*International Herald Tribune*)

A report on 22 July said that the Habibie government was offering subsidies on newsprint to publications in financial difficulty - in exchange for journalists submitting to a system of licensing. The president of the World Association of Newspapers, Bengt Braun, wrote to President Habibie: 'We respectfully remind you that any licensing is open to abuse

and almost inevitably leads to censorship or self-censorship.' (WAN, World Press Freedom Commitee)

IRAN

On 10 June 10 the moderate daily *Jameah*, which had been the object of virulent accusations by conservatives (*Index* 4/1998), was ordered to suspend publication and was fined 16 million rials (US$5,300). Editor **Hamid Reza Jalai Pour** was deprived of the right to 'exercise his functions' for one year by the special court which deals with 'offences' by the press. Another daily, *Gozarech e Rouz*, ceased publication after it was brought before the court to answer charges related to the reprinting of an article from an Arabic newspaper on how certain Iranian leaders had started remitting capital abroad. (RSF)

On 30 June an independent legal scholar, **Mohssen Saidzadeh**, was detained at his home and then taken to an undisclosed destination by plainclothes security officers. A leading figure in the campaign for the reform of family law, his reinterpretation of *sharia* in the controversial areas of personal status and women's rights was perceived as a threat to religious conservatives. He is also a writer for the *Jameah* newspaper, recently shut down by the government. (Lawyers Committee for Human Rights)

As the high-profile trial of Teheran's reformist mayor **Golamhossein Karbaschi** had its fourth hearing on 30

June, conservatives impeached another moderate in President Khatami's team, interior minister **Abdollah Nouri**, who had made key appointments which had displaced conservatives. Next on the conservative's hit list are said to be Aytaollah Mohajerani, the Islamic guidance minister and Foreign Minister Kamal Kharazzi, whose liberal policies have angered conservatives. (Lawyers Committee for Human Rights)

On 21 July **Ruhulla Rouhani**, a member of the Baha'i faith, was executed on charges of converting a Muslim woman to his religion. The woman concerned was not arrested and has claimed that she has always been a Baha'i. (AI)

On 29 July, publisher **Mohammed Reza Zaeri** of the weekly *Khaneh* was arrested and imprisoned in Teheran on two charges. The first was publishing a photograph of an unveiled woman 'contrary to public morals'. The other was printing a letter from a teenager, who said he did not know anything of Ayatollah Khomeini because he was only 12 when the leader died. Zaeri could face up to two years on charges of 'insulting Islam, the Shiite clergy and Ayatollah Khomeini'. (RSF)

On 2 August, another pro-democracy daily, *Aftab'e Emrooz* (The Sun Today), was launched despite the risk from hard-liners. *Jameah* was shut down in June and *Tous*, an imprint which arose from the ashes using the same journalists and design, was closed down by the judiciary on 1 August. Staff at *Aftab'e Emrooz* said they intended to ensure the continuation of frank criticism and analysis of domestic affairs. (*International Herald Tribune*)

ISRAEL

In late June, police raided the office of a Jewish settlers' pirate radio station, Channel 7, in the latest round of tension with the government. The station had been allowed to operate by successive government for fear of provoking a right-wing backlash over the issue of returning land to the Palestinians. (*Guardian*)

Several Knesset members demanded in late June that legal immunity be lifted from fellow deputy **Saleh Tarif** so that he could prosecuted for defamation over remarks against the influx of former settlers into Jerusalem. (*Jerusalem Times*)

Journalists are to be interrogated for allegedly breaking military censorship by publishing leaks that a Mossad agent had fabricated his reports from Syria, state-owned Channel One television announced on 3 July. Attorney-General Elyakim Rubinstein has reportedly ordered police to examine the performance of military censors and to question senior officials suspected of leaking details of the affair in December 1997. Mossad's reputation was further tarnished by the discosure that veteran agent Yehuda Gil had fed the spy agency false information for years and that

he pocketed money intended for informers. Gil pleaded not guilty at a closed-door trial. (Reuters)

Labour Knesset member **Nissim Zvili** alleged on 13 July that Prime Minister Netanyahu had met with a judge presiding over the trial of businessman Nahum Manbar, who was convicted in June of supplying Iran with material to produce nerve gas and to build munitions plants for chemical warheads from 1990 to 1995. The case was subject to reporting restrictions and the state prosecutor later ordered police to probe censorship violations. Government whip Meir Sheetrit accused Zvili of 'exploiting his parliamentary immunity' to breach the gag order. (Reuters)

Two Druse men were stabbed on 19 July, after apparently speaking Arabic together. The men, apparently mistaken for Palestinians, were attacked in Nahariya, near the Lebanese border. (*Jerusalem Times*)

At a 2 August High Court hearing, the state attorney agreed to allow the Gaza-based Palestinian journalist **Taher Shriteh** to travel abroad, but the presiding judges refused to rule on Shriteh's exclusion from Israel, referring the matter instead to the joint Israeli-Palestinian security committee which has not met for seven months. Shriteh, who reports for Reuters, CBS News and the *New York Times*, has been confined to Gaza by the security service Shin Bet for the past four years (*Index* 4/1998). The state attorney

argued that Shriteh posed 'a danger to the security of the country and the region' because he was 'an active Hamas member who carried out various tasks for the group'. Shriteh maintained in an affidavit that his only contact with Hamas had been as an interviewer. (CPJ, Reuters)

Recent Publications: *1987-1997—A decade of human rights violations* (B'Tselem, January 1998, 35pp); *Routine torture—Interrogation methods of the General Security Service* (B'Tselem, February 1998, 76pp); *Divide and rule—Prohibition on passage between the Gaza Strip and the West Bank* (B'Tselem, May 1998, 35pp); *Violations of International Labour Office conventions regarding the employment conditions of foreign migrant workers in Israel* (Kav La'Oved, June 1998, 16pp)

ITALY

In early July art experts criticised a film portrayal of the life of 17th-century Florentine painter Artemisia Gentileschi. *Artemisia: the Untold True Story of an Extraordinary Woman* depicts her as the willing lover of perspective teacher Agostino Tassi. The historical view is that Gentileschi was raped by Tassi. During his trial she underwent torture to validate her accusations. (*European, Guardian*)

Fiat chairman Ceasare Romiti stepped down in mid-June, taking as a retirement present Rizzoli, the editorial group that controls *Corriere della Sera*, Italy's largest-selling daily. It has been rumoured that Romiti intends to enter politics. (*European*)

JAPAN

Gynaecologist **Yahiro Netsu**, who had performed *in vitro* fertilisation procedures, was expelled from the nation's leading obstetric society on 27 June, sparking a national debate on a topic long considered too private or taboo for public discussion. 'I am ashamed the government shuts its eyes to this issue,' said Netsu. Yoshiaki Sawada, a doctor at a fertility clinic in Tokyo, believes 'there will probably come a time surrogate mothers or donor eggs are permitted' but children born by the method might be considered 'semi-orphans'. (*International Herald Tribune*)

Thirteen people were arrested on 6 July on suspicion of distributing pornography on the Internet. **Keiki Usui,** a computer consultant, and others were suspected of selling computers installed with software to post photography on websites with an in-built, pay-for-use telephone service. Although the 1,833 pornographic images found came with the legally required censorship mosaics to obscure images of genitalia, the sites provided software to remove them. (*Asahi Shimbun*)

JORDAN

On 6 June King Hussain stuck firmly to every provision of the new press and publication law in his meeting with the members of the press. The draft law, presented to the Chamber of Deputies in the third week of June, gives the information ministry powers to deny newspaper licences without the right to appeal, allows the press department a free hand in suing publications and closing them within 24 hours and raises the start-up capital which a newspaper requires from 50,000 dinars (US$70,000) to one million dinars (US$1.4 m). Dailies would have to deposit a bank guarantee of 100,000 dinars at the information ministry, and weeklies 50,000 dinars, to ensure payment of 'future fines incurred'. The law also includes pre-publication censorship and the prohibition of foreign publications. Condemning the draft law as an assault on free expression, 12 opposition parties and 13 professional bodies said it 'transgresses citizens' rights and degrades Jordan's reputation'. Writing in the daily *al-Rai*, Fahed Fanek said the regulations had been brought in by 'a government living in isolation that does not really know about the media business' and would mean the death of audio and visual media. (HRW, A19, Reuters)

On 8 August, parliament ratified a press law which includes wide-ranging prohibitions on disparaging coverage of King Hussein or his family, information about the armed forces and articles that could harm the stability of the dinar, undermine national unity, degrade religion or morals, damage an individual's reputation or give information about secret parliamentary sessions. (Reuters)

KENYA

Kwendo Opanga, political columnist at the *Nation,* resigned on 24 June following his own admission that he had breached the paper's policies. Opanga admitted he had been hired for an unspecified sum of money by the ruling party, Kanu, to help its strategies for the 1992 elections. Opanga claimed he had been under pressure to leave the independent *Nation*, which is considered an opposition paper, but added that he was threatened with death by party lobbyists who wanted him to stay. (*Nation*)

On 1 July, the weekly *Post on Sunday* was restrained by the High Court from publishing any articles discussing businessman Joshua Kulei. (NDIMA)

In early July, **Magayu Kiarie Magayu**, editor in chief, and general manager **Francis Mathenge Wanderitwo** of the opposition paper *Star* appeared in court charged with publishing an 'alarmist' article entitled 'How coup was to be executed'. They were released on bail and will appear in court again on 8 September. The *Star* is also being sued for libel by Deputy State House Controller John Lokorio, following an article on 23 June entitled 'Moi loses grip on State House - Kipsigis flushed out as VP race hots up' and also for another published on 30 June: 'State bosses defy Nyachae order'. (NDIMA, *West Africa*)

The editor of the *Post on Sunday*, **Tony Gachoka**, had to lock himself in his office to avoid being arrested by 10 plainclothes police on 8 July. Area CID boss Henry Nyaosi said he wanted Gachoka 'for a chat'. (NDIMA)

Also on 8 July, *Nation* journalist **Esther Mwangi** was assualted by the owner of a girls' school in the Nakuru district. Mwangi had gone to the school to cover a student strike. (NDIMA)

On 10 July registration applications from the *Star*, *Finance* and *Post on Sunday* publications were rejected by the authorities, effectively banning them. A fourth publication, *Kenya Confidential*, was declared illegal for not having applied for registration, in spite of claims by owner **Blamuel Njururi** that his application last November had never been answered. *Star* editor **Magayu K. Magayu**, detained at Kasarani police station on 8 July for publishing an 'alarming' article, was released on 10 July and immediately rearrested. The managing director of Star Publishers Ltd, **Francis Mathenge Wanderi**, was also charged on the same count. Both were released on US$3,000 bonds.

Nation correspondent **Imanene Imathiu** was beaten badly and treated in hospital for injuries on 10 July. Imathiu had been among a team of journalists who had talked to local adminstration officials regarding allegations of corruption at a local police camp. His camera was also

damaged. (NDIMA)

The next day, youths seized and burned copies of the *Nation* in Nairobi after the Nation Media Group was threatened by members of the opposition party, the NDP. The youths said: 'We cannot allow this newspaper to spoil our name. Our co-operation with Kanu should not be interfered with.' On 10 July, the pro-government *Kenya Times* ran a story which quoted a NDP MP accusing the *Nation* of 'evolving a cryptic editorial policy, bordering on ethnic chauvinism, that seeks to cast (the) NDP, its leader Raila Odinga and the party's MPs in a negative light'. (NDIMA)

On 13 July, Star Publishers Ltd went to court to have the decision to reject the newspaper's registration quashed. The next day police confiscated copies of the paper but editions of all four banned papers were on sale on 21 July, although vendors were apprehensive of the consequences. On 31 July, the High Court withdrew charges against *Post on Sunday*, allowing the paper to resume publication, and the *Star* also continued to publish. (IPI, NDIMA, RSF, *Nation*)

On 14 July *Daily Nation* journalist **Said Wabera** received anonymous telephone death threats which instructed him to 'know what you should and should not write'. The calls followed Wabera's research on the status of Oromo Liberation Front guerillas hiding on the Kenya-Ethiopia border. (NDIMA)

KYRGYZSTAN

On 12 June Tursunbai Bakir, member of parliament and chair of the government's Commission on Human Rights, announced in the government newspaper *Slovo Kyrgyzstan* his intention to seek compensation for 'moral losses' from Aleksei Sukhov, a journalist for the independent *Res Publica*. Writing about Bakir's involvement in local by-elections in Osh at the beginning of June, Sukhov said that the electors would not have voted for his protégé if they had known about Bakir's links with the drug trade. (Bureau on Human Rights and Rule of Law)

On 23 June the legislature passed amendments to the law on the media. The changes allow any state or local administrative body, member of parliament or local council, and state officials the right to demand that the media publish a reply or a commentary to an article which, in their opinion, does not reflect the 'reality' of an issue. (Bureau on Human Righs and Rule of Law)

LEBANON

On 24 July the Beirut military tribunal sentenced **Pierre Attalah**, a journalist with *an-Nahar*, to three years' imprisonment and a fine of 500,000 Lebanese pounds (US$330). In December 1996 he was questioned about an interview with Etienne Saqr, a former head of the 'Cedar Guards', who was under sentence of death for 'secret dealings with the Israeli enemy'. (RSF)

MALAWI

In June the government criticised the newly launched weekly *National Agenda,* saying it had carried stories whichwere 'untrue, insulting and inflammatory' to the public and to President Bakili Muluzi. Information Minister Sam Mpasu blamed opposition leaders for taking advantage of the 'existing press freedom'. (MISA)

MALAYSIA

It was reported on 14 July that that the group editor-in-chief of *Utusan Melayu,* **Johan Jaafar,** had resigned 'under political pressure from the government'. His resignation came two weeks after the Mahathir government criticised the local press for 'negative' reporting on Kuala Lumpur's new airport. Four days later, **Ahmad Nazri Abdullah,** group editor of the largest-circulation newspaper *Berita Harian,* resigned. Mahathir denied that he had anything to do with their decisions. (*International Herald Tribune, Daily Telegraph,* CPF)

It was reported on 23 July that the Deputy Home Minister Tajol Rosli threatened to jail without trial two people who allegedly supplied news organisations with pictures of riots at Seminyah, a detention centre for illegal immigrants from Indonesia. (Associated Press, *International Herald Tribune*)

According to a report on 27

July, Deputy Information Minister Suleiman Mohamad threatened to jail journalists without trial if they continued using the economic crisis to 'undermine the country's leadership'. 'If the media indulges in activities that threaten political stability or national unity,' he warned, 'we will come down hard, regardless of whether they are local or foreign.' (*Sun, Far East Economic Review,* RSF)

MALDIVES

On 21 June *Haveeru* reported that **Anne sa Hussain** and **Aminath Moonisa** had been arrested three days earlier for spreading Christianity, a 'serious offence' according to M. Zahir, First Secretary at the High Commission in Colombo. On 28 July the Evangelical Alliance of Sri Lanka claimed that 50 Christians had subsequently been imprisoned because of their beliefs. (*Sunday Leader,* Reuters)

MAURITANIA

On 10 June the latest edition of the Arab-language paper *La Tribune* was censored for the fifth time in less than a month, with no explanation. Editor **Mohammed Fall Oumere** said: 'We already practise self-censorship. Now they want to make us disappear.' (RSF)

MEXICO

On 5 June photographer **Pascual Gorriz** of the Associated Presse was threatened by police in Chiapas. In April the

photographer and a journalist from Agence France Press were beaten for covering the expulsion of a group of foreign human rights observers (*Index* 4/1998). (CPJ)

Following a battle between the army and the members of the Revolutionary Popular Army on 7 June, in which 11 people were killed, the authorities sealed off the area to journalists for 24 hours. Three days later foreign journalists were still not allowed to enter. (CPJ)

On 28 June journalist **Paige Bierna** was forced off the bus as she returned from a student gathering to commemorate the massacre of 17 peasants in Guerrero. She was told to appear in front of immigration authorities the next morning, despite having the required journalist visa and press pass. (CPJ)

NAMIBIA

On 23 July, after researching a story on a private Catholic school, a journalist and a cameraman from the NBC corporation were assaulted by the school manager and charged with trespass. **Unomengi Kauapirura** and cameraman **Hadley Mwashekeleh** have laid charges of assault against the manager of Ginichas Junior Secondary School, Phillipus Pollitzer. (MISA)

NEPAL

Policemen in Kathmandu told transport firms on 2 July not to handle newspapers that publish reports on their operations against Maoist Communist Party of Nepal rebels. Since 9 June newspapers, which published stories about security forces' operations against the guerrillas, have had their print runs seized. (RSF, AI)

NEW ZEALAND

A book by former MP **Michael Laws** has been twice recalled after a television political editor claimed defamation. Laws' political memoir, *The Demon Profession*, was due to be released on 21 May, but it was postponed when TVNZ's Linda Clark threatened to sue. A settlement was reached when it was agreed that a non-removable sticker would be placed over a nine-line paragraph which referred to Clark. But the stickers proved easy to remove and the book has again been pulled from shelves. (New Zealand Press Association)

Police in Tokoroa are seeking legal advice over 'Nga Pou Pou Korero', an eight-foot Maori statue with an erect penis that has been called obscene by National Heritage Party leader Revd Graham Capill, the force behind protests at a Wellington art exhibition in February . (*New Zealand News UK*)

NIGERIA

Two journalists, **Oladipo Adelowo** and **Modupe Olubanjo**, and photojournalist **Alaba Igbaroola**, of *Tribune on Saturday*, were assaulted on 20 June by aides of Ibadan-based politician Alhaji Lamidi Adedibu. The journalists had gone to Adedibu's house to

seek an interview with him on the current political situation. He became irked by the journalists' questions and they were assaulted, verbally abused and had their recording confiscated, prior to being chased from the house. ('IPR')

Moshood Abiola, president-elect and a prominent publisher, died in custody on 7 July on the eve of his release from five years in prison mostly spent in solitary confinement. (IPI)

Niran Malaolu, (*Index* 2/1998, 3/1998, 4/1998), editor of the *Diet* newspaper, had his life sentence reduced to 15 years on 7 July. He was sentenced to life imprisonment in April for 'information gathering' into the alleged December 1997 coup. The death sentence passed on former Chief of the General Staff Lt.Gen. Oladipo Diya was also commuted to 25 years in prison, and five other coup suspects had life sentences reduced to 15 years. (CPJ)

On 15 July **Adetokunbo Fakeye**, defence correspondent of *PM News*, and **Rafui Salau**, administrative manager of the *News/Tempo/PM News* group, were released from detention. Fakeye and Salau were arrested in November 1997. Fakeye disappeared while on assignment at Army Defence headquarters in Lagos. Salau was arrested at the directorate of Military Intelligence, where he had gone to enquire about Fakeye (*Index* 1/1998). (CPJ)

Three journalists serving 15 years in prison were released on

20 July. *News* editor **Kunle Ajibade**, *Tell* magazine's assistant editor **George Mba** and former editor of the now defunct *Classique* magazine **Ben Charles Obi**, were convicted as 'accessories to the fact of treason' for stories their publications carried on the alleged 1995 coup (*Index* 3/1995, 4/1995). (CPJ, 'IPR')

Babafemi Ojudu, managing director of *News* and *Tempo* magazines (*Index* 1/1998), was released on 23 July, apparently in response to alerts that he was dying in detention. Ojudu was rushed to hospital, where he is being treated for typhoid and jaundice. ('IPR')

On the weekend of 25-26 July, three Ondo State Television (ODTV) journalists were reinstated. **Rotimi Obamuwagun**, **Sehinde Adeniyi** and **Ola Bamidele** were sacked in May for 'disloyalty and subversive activities against government' after they issued a press release condemning the assault of ODTV general manager Dunni Fagbayibo by unidentified soldiers (*Index* 4/1998). ('IPR')

On 28 July journalists covering the launch of the new United Nigeria Peoples Party (UNPP) were assaulted and had cameras smashed when they tried to take pictures of the party leader, Alhaji Isa Mohammed, who had slumped during his keynote speech. The incident led to a brawl between journalists and politicians. ('IPR')

Ofonime Umanah, Anambra state correspondent of *Punch*

newspaper, was taken by police on 29 July and detained at Enugwu Ukwu police post. They gave no reasons for his detention. (IJC)

PAKISTAN

On 9 July a bomb exploded at the Karachi bureau of the daily *Dawn*. Half an hour earlier, another blast took place near the offices. Majid Nizami, president of the All Pakistan Newspaper Society, speculated that the blasts were a warning to stop exposing the motives of a recent spate of terrorism, which has officially been blamed on India. (Pakistan Press Foundation)

On 19 July **Ansar Naqvi**, bureau chief of the *News*, and **M.H. Khan**, correspondent for *Dawn*, were assaulted at a police checkpoint in Hyderabad. (Pakistan Press Foundation)

On 24 July the father of exiled journalist **Khalid H. Lodhi** (*Index* 6/1996) was detained for over 24 hours, and his Faisalabad home raided by local police and internal security agents. He was told that his son, currently seeking asylum in the UK, would be charged in his absence with 'anti-state activities'. Lodhi believes that the raid was connected to his work on a book about high-level government corruption. All documents, books and photos relevant to the book, Lodhi said, were seized by the authorities from his father's house. (*Newham Recorder, Daily Jang, Nation*)

Recent Publication: *Mohajirs of*

Pakistan: Plight and struggle for survival by Rashid Jamal (Loh-e-Adab, May 1998)

PERU

On 25 May the tabloid *el Tio* published an article headlined 'The traitor Paez sends secret army documents abroad', part of a campaign by the pro-government press to defame **Angel Paez,** investigative journalist with the newspaper *La República* (*Index* 3/1998, 4/1998). Four newspapers specialising in soft pornography and crime - *El Chino, El Mananero, El Tio* and *La Chuchi* - have published articles on a daily basis for two months which accuse Paez of being a liar and a 'merchant of state secrets'. Though the papers all have separate staffs, the articles are often printed with identical headlines. The campaign began after the publication of articles by Paez on arms trafficking, bribery and government purchases of overpriced armaments. (*New York Times, Independent, International Herald Tribune*)

On 18 June TV Channel 13 received a fax threatening journalist and current affairs presenter **Cesar Hildebrandt** and journalist **Luis Iberico**. The messages - read on air by Hildelbrandt - stated that both were under close surveillance and their safety was in jeopardy. (AI)

The offices of the Association for Human Rights (APRODEH) received a fax on 19 June accusing director, **Francisco Soberon** and opposition parliamentarian

Javier Diez Canseco of being 'accomplices of terrorism'. Soberon was also accused of assisting police captain Julio Salas Caceres and army intelligence officer Luisa Zanatta to flee the country after they had denounced corruption and human rights violations by the security forces. (AI)

On 30 June Attorney General Hugo Salvatierra heard testimony from **Mirko Lauer**, political columnist for *La República,* one of several journalists whose telephones had been tapped. Lauter answered questions for over an hour, mainly related to his daily column *El Observador,* one most critical of the government. (Instituto de Prensa y Sociedad)

A new criminal trial against **Baruch Ivcher** on charges of tax evasion commenced on 30 June. Formerly majority owner of Frecuencia Latina television, Ivcher has been deprived of his nationality and hounded into exile (*Index* 4/1997, 5/1997, 6/1997, 2/1998, 3/1998, 4/1998). ((Instituto de Prensa y Sociedad)

POLAND

Former Warsaw police chief **Marek Papala** was shot dead on 25 June. Although he resigned earlier this year, it was suspected that his murder was in retaliation for his work combating organised crime. While denying any influence from the murder, the Interior Ministry announced on 29 June that troops would return to the streets of Warsaw for the first time since the introduction of martial law in 1981. (RFE/RL)

ROMANIA

On 25 June the Senate approved by 109-7 a law to open the former secret police files, provided this did not affect 'national security'. While the law, yet to be approved by the Chamber of Deputies, will establish a National Council for the Study of the Archives of the Former Securitate, it leaves files with the Intelligence Service and the ministries of defence and justice. The council can apply to see information from these bodies, but cannot store the files itself. (RFE/RL)

RUSSIA

On 23 June the private network NTV, owned by Vladimir Gusinskii, cancelled the morning talk show *Chas byka* after host **Andrei Cherkizov**, referred to Belarus President Lukashenka as a 'boor'. Informed by one of Lukashenka's aides that NTV could be cut off in the state, an NTV newscaster apologised to the president on air. Next morning, however, Cherkizov called Lukashenka a 'swine', provoking NTV to cancel the programme. NTV has a history of strained relations with Lukashenka, but they appeared to have improved after Gusinskii and the media magnate Boris Berezovskii visited the president in January. (RFE/RL)

On 24 June it was announced that the Supreme Court would

hear journalist **Galina Tuz's** appeal against a Stavropol Krai court ruling that she libelled the national-socialist group Russian National Unity (RNE) in *Stavropolskaya Pravda*. The RNE won a lawsuit forcing the paper's editorial office to pay a fee and publish an apology after an article, published in 1996, was found to have damaged its business reputation by suggesting that the party appeared 'in essence a fascist organisation' and pursued 'a fascist ideology'. Tuz's lawyer claims arguments for the defence were ignored in court. (RFE/RL)

On 29 June **Sergei Bachinin**, editor in chief of *Vyatsky Nablyudatel*, was found semi-conscious in his apartment, suffering from a fractured skull. The attack is one more in a long line of assaults and harassment, linked to his profession as editor of a paper renowned for criticisng the local authorities. (Glasnost Defence Foundation, RFE/RL)

On the same day, State Customs Committee head Valerii Draganov requested that Prime Minister Sergei Kirienko dismiss three deputy heads of the committee: **Valerii Shpagin**, **Valerii Maksimtsev** and **Nikolai Lyutov**. His request came in response to an open letter by 15 editors to President Yeltsin, which slammed the activities of customs officials. In February the committee tried to charge VAT on print media published abroad, although this was deemed illegal by the Supreme Court in June. The following

week, officials held up issues of several magazines, demanding proof they were cultural, scientific, or educational in nature. The law on state support for the mass media exempts all print media from VAT, except for publications devoted to advertising or erotica. (RFE/RL)

Police have arrested a fourth suspect in the murder of **Larisa Yudinka**, editor-in-chief of *Sovietskaya Kalmykia Segodnya* (*Index* 4/1998). Sergei Lipin was incriminated during the investigation of one of the three other suspects. He is accused of moving Yudinka's body after the murder to the pond where it was found. He has allegedly confessed to his part in the crime, but insists he does not know who gave the order to kill the journalist. (RFE/RL)

On 3 July **Lev Rokhlin**, former chairman of the state defence committee, was shot dead at his *dacha*. Although Rokhlin's wife confessed to his murder soon after, a number of conspiracy theories emerged including that of Vladimir Zhironovsky, leader of the Liberal Democratic Party (LDP) who suggested that he was killed because 'he knew too much about Chechnya'. On 5 July relatives of Tamara Rokhlin claimed she had been pressured into confessing to her husband's murder. It was reported that, when first interviewed about her husband's murder, she was in a state of shock and not accompanied by a lawyer. Aleksandr Morozov, deputy head of Rokhlin's Movement to Support the Army, vowed to sue those who have publicly accused Tamara of her husband's murder, but on 10 July, she was formally charged with the murder. (RFE/RL)

On 3 July **Igor Rudnikov**, editor-in-chief of the Kalingrad newspaper *Noviye Kolysa*, was attacked with an iron pipe. Rudnikov, who is also a deputy on the Kalingrad City Council, is in a extremely serious condition with severe head injuries. His colleagues suspect the attack may be in relation to the paper's articles about the governor of the region. (Glasnost Defence Foundation, RSF)

On 21 July it was reported that four ethnic Russians arrested in the Osh region of Kyrgyzstan had confessed to the August 1997 murder of St Petersburg deputy governor and privatisation chief **Mikhail Manevich**. The group are also suspected of the March 1995 murder of television journalist **Vladislav Listev**, as part of a series of contract killings. (RFE/RL)

RWANDA

On 1 July the government rejected the latest UN human rights report, which detailed evidence of current and former army involvement in massacres in eastern former- Zaire and and the Congolese government's attempts to cover them up. The government said that it 'categorically rejected and was deeply shocked by the insinuation in the report'. (IRIN)

The UN announced on 17 July that it would withdraw from the state because the government refused to allow its observers to monitor and report effectively. (Reuters)

On 19 July four people were convicted on charges of genocide and two were sentenced to death. Euphrasie Kamantu was convicted of organising the killings of minority Tutsi and moderate Hutu in Kigali during the 1994 genocide. She and husband Thomas Habyarimana were found guilty of distributing weapons to killing squads, writing up death lists and manning roadblocks so that Tutsi could not escape. The other two received life sentences. (*International Herald Tribune*)

SAMOA

Observer editor-publisher **Savea Sano Malifa** must pay approximately £10,000 in damages to Prime Minister Tofilau Eti Alesana, after losing a defamation case that the politician brought against him (*Index* 4/1997, 5/1997, 6/1997, 1/1998, 3/1998, 4/1998). Malifa has already paid about £45,000 in legal fees, while the premier's fees, amounting to some £150,000, have been added to the country's 1998-99 budget. Malifa still faces criminal charges over the same incident and may have to sell the *Observer*, the island's only independent daily newspaper, to cover his legal debts. (PINA)

SERBIA-MONTENEGRO

Radio Kontakt, the first independent radio station in Kosovo, was launched on 21 June, broadcasting in Albanian, Serbian and Roma. Having submitted the necessary documents for a licence, the editor-in-chief, **Doria Nuay,** was visited by an inspector of the Telecommunications Ministry, accompanied by fully armed policemen, who imposed a ban three days later for operating wtihout a licence. The transmitter was seized, despite a note from the ministry confirming the station's licence application was in order. (B92, RSF)

On 26 June independent Radio B92 began proceedings against the Federal Telecommunications Ministry for declining to sign a contract for a frequency licence issued to the station in the recent open competition (*Index* 4/1998). The station's legal suit claims the ministry is obliged to provide an explanation for this, and why it refused to grant two other licences applied for. (B92)

On 31 June, state-controlled Radio Belgrade accused foreign journalists of writing lies about the state and openly supporting the Kosovo Liberation Army (KLA).The station singled out CNN's **Christiane Amapour** as having falsified information to 'blame the Serbian side'. (B92, ANEM)

On 6 July two British journalists were beaten by plain-clothes Serbian police near the village of Prekaz. **Kurt Schork** of Reuters was punched in the face and *The Times'* **Anthony Lloyd** received two broken ribs. The reporters were part of a convoy following the international envoys and media around villages destroyed in the conflict. The incident is part of a pattern of harassment against journalists (*Index*, 4/1998). In June a Danish TV2 crew were fired upon by Serbian soldiers. (CPJ)

On 13 July Radio B92 signed a contract with the Ministry of Telecommunications for the use of its radio frequency. It had previously refused to do so until its monthly fee had been reduced by 50 per cent (*Index* 4/1998). (B92)

On 16 July the first completely independent distribution network for newspapers began operating. The joint venture between the World Association of Newspapers (WAN) and Unesco is run by a new Belgrade-based distribution company and intends to free the press from the government domination of distribution. (WAN)

On 18 July three armed individuals, presumed members of the KLA, attacked **Sergei Mitine**, correspondent with Moscow's daily *Izvestia*, as he travelled in a vehicle with Belgrade plates on the Glogovac-Srbica route. Despite showing his passport and accreditation at the KLA roadblock, he was accused of being a Serbian spy and taken to a house where he was beaten for several hours. His

film and camera confiscated, he was abandoned on the road to Prishtina. (RSF)

On 20 July independent media association ANEM launched a protest against the jamming of Belgrade's independent Radio Index. The Telecommunications Ministry had instructed Radio Bon-Ton and Radio Top FM to relocate their frequencies near the 88.90FM band used by Radio Index to make space for a new station. Since no station is broadcasting between 88.10 and 88.90, the ministry's directive has been interpreted as a means of stifling independent opinion. (ANEM)

On 22 July, President Milosevic and his wife attended the launch of TV Kosava, part of his daughter's media empire. TV Kosava was not reportedly one the stations granted a frequency in the recent tender (*Index* 4/1998). (AMARC)

SIERRA LEONE

On 3 June, the Income Tax Department announced a 383 per cent increase in tax assessments on publishers for the 1998 fiscal year. All print media, whether operational or not during the 10-month junta which ended last February, are being charged on the assumption that they were publishing daily. (CPJ)

Joseph Mboka, editor of the *Democrat*, was arrested in connection with a story entitled 'Danger, Sanko to return' in late June, while the arrest of **Jonathan Leigh**, managing editor of the

Independent Observer, was linked to a story regarding the army's recruitment of 3,000 former junta soldiers. **Ahmed Kanneh**, of *Newstorm*, violated the emergency laws by publishing an article on a suspected ECOMOG murder suspect. (CPJ)

Foday Fofana and **Alusine Fofana**, journalists with the *Star* newspaper, appeared before a magistrate court in Freetown on 14 July charged with publishing 'defamatory, libellous and false reports likely to disturb the public'. On 15 July **Umaru David** and **David Konteh**, journalists with the *Champion* newspaper, appeared in the same court on the same charges. The journalists were forced to pay bail and their case was adjourned to 5 August.

SINGAPORE

The Film and Publicity Department announded on 13 July a review of the long-banned films *The Year of Living Dangerously*, about the 1965 Communist uprising in Indonesia, and *Beyond Ragoon*, a human rights drama set in Burma. (Reuters)

The Court of Appeal announced on 23 July that it was quintupling the damages awarded to Prime Minister Goh Chok Tong in his defamation suit against opposition leader J.B. Jeyaretnam (*Index* 6/1997). Jeyaretnam was ordered to pay all Goh's costs and a fine of £35,000. (*Far East Economic Review, Guardian*)

SOUTH AFRICA

On 27 June **Thabo Mabaso**, a *Cape Argus* journalist, was allegedly beaten by 10 policeman at the Gugulethu police station after reporting a traffic accident. He was taken to hospital for treatment, but has since lost the sight in his left eye. (Freedom of Expression Institute)

On 13 July the national Child Welfare Council pressed charges against artist **Mark Hipper** for his exhibition exploring child sexuality at the country's main arts festival. (Freedom of Expression Institute)

SOUTH KOREA

The Ministry of Culture and Tourism announced on 1 July that prior screening of films and theatrical work would be abolished and replaced with a rating system according to their content. This move is part of a reform package aimed as halving the 622 regulations governing the performing arts, publishing and broadcasting *(Korea Times)*

The recently-published *Eroticism in Korean Art History* by Professor Lee Tae-ho finds that, unlike contemporary attitudes towards sex, ancient Koreans had a candid stance towards it and openly expressed it. Other compilations of art eroticism have usually been censored. (*Korean Times*)

SPAIN

National newspaper *ABC* published on 15 June a racist article on the eve of the World Cup match between Nigeria and Spain, which referred to the Ku-Klux-Klan and claimed the World Cup is full of 'negritos', whom the writer compare with Basques. (*ABC*)

The radical separatist Basque newspaper *Egin* and Egin Irratia radio station were closed on 16 July under an order given by Judge Baltasar Garzón. The newspaper and radio station are closely linked with the terrorist group ETA and are alleged to have cooperated in their actions. (*El Pais*)

On the night of 16 July the office of Basque radio station Cadena Ser in San Sebastian was bombed causing major damage. Two nights later another Basque radio station, Cadena Cope, suffered a similar attack in the same city. The attacks were perpetrated by Basque militants protesting the closure of the *Egin* newspaper after it was accused of supporting the armed group ETA. (RSF)

Former Socialist interior minister Jose Barrionuevo was sentenced to 10 years' imprisonment in late July. While cleared of actually setting up the Anti-Terrorist Liberation Groups, said to be responsible for 28 murders during the 1980s, he was implicated in the covert war undertaken against ETA by the authorities. (*European, Guardian*)

SRI LANKA

On 17 June at least 40 T56 anti-tank bullets were fired at the house of **Lasantha Wickrematunge**, editor of the *Sunday Leader*. Wickrematunge, who has been openly critical of the government and alleged corruption by Media and Telecommunications Minister Mangala Samaraweera, had just returned home when an unknown number of individuals opened fire from a van. (AI, Reuters, Free Media Movement)

In the aftermath of a historic Colombo High Court judgement on 3 July, in which security forces personnel were found guilty of human rights violations against Tamils and sentenced to death, Tamil politicians urged the government to investigate the claims of Corporal Dewage Somaratne and his five co-defendants that they had buried hundreds of murdered Tamils in the Jaffna peninsula since 1996. (AI, Tamil Informtion Centre, Reuters)

On 16 July **Sri Gajan**, a journalist with the Tamil-language daily *Virakesari*, was detained by police in Colombo on 'suspicion' and 'connections with the LTTE' (Liberation Tigers Of Tamil Eelam). On 20 July another *Virakesari* correspondent and BBC and Reuters stringer **Ponniah Manickavasagam**, along with Tamil journalist **K. Theivanayagam**, were also taken into custody. (Reuters, SWB, Agence France Presse, RSF, Free Media Movement, A19, CPJ, *Hindustan Times, The Sunday Times*)

Simon Davies on

PRIVACY

Patricia Williams on

RACE

Gabriel Garcia Marquez on

JOURNALISM

Edward Lucie-Smith on

THE INTERNET

Ursula Owen on

HATE SPEECH

...all in INDEX

SUBSCRIBE & SAVE

UK and overseas

○ **Yes! I want to subscribe to *Index*.**

❐ 1 year (6 issues)   £39   Save 28%
❐ 2 years (12 issues)   £74   Save 31%
❐ 3 years (18 issues)   £102   **You save 37%**

Name

Address

B8B4

£ _____ enclosed. ❑ Cheque (£) ❑ Visa/MC ❑ Am Ex ❑ Bill me
(*Outside of the UK, add £6 a year for foreign postage*)

Card No.

Expiry   Signature

❑ I do not wish to receive mail from other companies.

INDEX ON CENSORSHIP

✉ Freepost: INDEX, 33 Islington High Street, London N1 9BR
☎ (44) 171 278 2313   Fax: (44) 171 278 1878
e   syra@indexoncensorship.org

SUBSCRIBE & SAVE

North America

○ **Yes! I want to subscribe to *Index*.**

❐ 1 year (6 issues) $52   Save 21%
❐ 2 years (12 issues) $96   Save 27%
❐ 3 years (18 issues) $135   **You save 32%**

Name

Address

B8B4

$ _____ enclosed. ❑ Cheque ($) ❑ Visa/MC ❑ Am Ex ❑ Bill me

Card No.

Expiry   Signature

❑ I do not wish to receive mail from other companies.

✉ INDEX, 708 Third Avenue, 8th Floor, New York, NY 10017
☎ (44) 171 278 2313   Fax: (44) 171 278 1878
e   syra@indexoncensorship.org

SUDAN

On 4 July, the authorities confiscated editions of the independent newspapers *Al-Rai Al Akbar* and *Al-Shari Al-Siyasi* from their publishing houses in Khartoum. Although no official explanation was given, it is believed that the action is connected with new directives issued by the National Press and Publications Council ordering newspapers not to criticise the new constitution.(RSF)

On 21 July the daily paper *Alwan* was suspended for two days following an article which criticised authorities for seizing the wheat harvest from farmers in eastern Sudan as a way of recovering debts. The Sudanese National Press and Publications Council (SNPPC) said that the daily had published a 'blasphemous' article. (RSF)

At the beginning of August, daily newspapers were obliged to raise their cover prices by 60 per cent, in response to a SNPPC ruling that publications should increase the number of pages to 12. 'Political papers' (general news) have been specifically targeted by the SNPPC, while sports and and arts papers are not affected (PANA)

SYRIA

In a 4 July interview, Syrian Journalists' Union head Saber Falhout rejected Article 19's claims in its report *Walls of Silence* that the state of emergency in effect since 1962 meant journalists were barred from reporting on a host of issues, including peace talks with Israel and the restructuring of the economy. The report said the laws, reinforced by the state monopoly on the media, make it illegal to 'disturb public confidence' or 'oppose the aims of the revolution' and that journalists breaking these codes face detention without trial, ill treatment while in custody and loss of their civil rights. Falhout maintained that 'there is no type of censorship in Syria. Journalists practise their jobs in accordance with their belief and their commitment to their profession and to their nation.' (Reuters)

Recent Publication: *Walls of silence - Media and censorship in Syria* (A19, June 1998, pp104)

TAJIKISTAN

On the evening of 8 June **Meirkhaim Gavrielov**, the editor-in-chief of the Tajik Agrarian University newspaper *Donish* and chairman of the Bukhara Jewish Cultural Society, was murdered by unknown persons who burst into his house and strangled him with wire. Law enforcement agencies have refused to comment on the murder but have, unofficially, spread rumours of suicide. (Glasnost Defence Foundation)

On 26 July President Rakhmonov banned beards in the army, a move that may cause displeasure among Islamist former guerillas being integrated into the force after last year's peace agreement to end the civil war. (Reuters)

On 27 July Igor Satarov, the Ministry of Foreign Affairs, revoked the accreditation of NTV's correspondant **Yelena Masyuk**. Masyuk was declared an 'undesirable' for having allegedly disseminated reports aimed at 'discrediting the government and its policies.' (RSF, RFE/RL, Glasnost Defence Foundation)

TANZANIA

Photo-journalist **Amour Nassor** of the state-owned weekly *Nuru* had his film confiscated by police in Zanzibar on 21 June, while covering voting in a parliamentary by-election. (MISA)

Two more privately owned newspapers, *Tishinga* and *Watu*, were banned at the end of June (*Index* 4/1998.) The official reason was that the papers had violated the Newspaper Act No. 3 of 1976 and the Newspaper Regulations of 1977, but the ban on *Tishinga* was probably prompted by its absorption of the recently banned paper *Kasheshe*. *Tishinga*'s front page had carried a cartoon with the caption: 'My condition is just as you can see it, to continue with good work that I have always been doing.' **Vumi Urasa**, owner of both papers, apologised to the government in early July. He claimed that the number of redundancies created by *Kasheshe* led to employees being rehired by *Tishinga*. Meanwhile, *Watu*, a revived defunct paper with the same owners as banned papers *Arusha Leo* and *Chombeza*, has also been prohbited for publishing so-called pornographic cartoons, an 'unregistered' change in editorial policy according to official sources. (MISA)

On the night of 30 June a fire destroyed the house of BBC correspondent **Nechi Lyimo**. The journalist and his family narrowly missed death when a petrol bomb was thrown into the house. On 3 July a police investigation was carried out by the Kilimanjaro regional commissioner, Philemon Sarungi. Earlier, on 12 June, two police detectives had questioned Lyimo following a controversial story in the weekly *Sanifu* about an assistant bishop who was allegedly having an affair with a married woman. The police have since called the interrogation a 'technical error'. (MISA)

A journalist at the private Dar es Salaam Television (DTV), **Betty Masanja**, was interrogated for over two hours on 30 July by police. She was forced to write a statement testifying to the association of vice-chairman of the Zanzibari-based Civic United Front (CUF) party Seif Shariff Hamad with charges of treason facing 18 other leading activists for the CUF. Masanja had interviewed Hamad on television in 1995. (MISA)

TUNISIA

Taoufik Ben Brik, a correspondent for *La Croix* and *Agence Periscoop Syfia*, was detained on 18 June and advised by Interior Ministry officials to 'find another job'. His recent article detailed the

practises of the *moudahamat*, or secret police. (IFJ)

Khemaïs Ksila, the jailed vice-president of the Human Rights Defence League, was reported to have restarted a hunger strike on 18 July, in protest at the lack of improvement in his conditions (*Index* 3/1998). Ksila was jailed for three years on 11 February for crimes including the 'distribution of false information' stemming from his publication of human rights abuses. (OMCT)

Recent Publication: *Surveillance and repression: freedom of expression in Tunisia* (A19, May 1998, pp114)

TURKEY

Hali Keskin, the owner of *Emek*, and editor **Ahmet Elgin** were each fined approximately £500 on 8 May for publishing details from the Public Prosecutor's notes on the case of one of the so-called 'disappeared', Kenan Bilgin (*Emek*)

In the ongoing trial of the editors of the Freedom of Thought books and campaign (*Index* 3/1998), the prosecution claimed that 'writing is more dangerous than supplying food and clothing to terrorists.' Journalists **Can Dunder**, **Mahmut Tali Ongoren**, **Temil Demirer** and **Varlik Ozmenek** face the same charges as academic **Haluk Gerger**, who was imprisoned earlier this year. (*Turkish Daily News*, Med-TV)

Two pro-Islamist journalists,

Yasar Kaplan and editor **Murat Balibey** of *Akit* newspaper, were accused on 5 June of 'inciting soldiers to break the law and disobey orders' in an article written in the daily. (Reuters)

Namik Durukan (*Index* 3/1998), journalist with *Milliyet* newspaper and the BBC, was acquitted on 10 June of helping the PKK. He had been charged on the evidence of an informer. (*Turkish Daily News*)

Kurdish daily *Ulkede Gundem* was confiscated on 10 June, following a State Security court decision that an article in the paper entitled 'Massacre on the border' 'incited people to enmity'. *Ulkede Gundem's* office in Batman was bombed on 21 June. (Med-TV, American Kurdish Information Network)

Forty-five students at Dicle University in southeast Turkey have been prevented from enrolling for the next academic year because they insist on wearing earrings, long hair and beards. (Med-TV)

On 16 July, the Appeals Court overturned a verdict which jailed five police officers for the murder of journalist **Metin Goktepe** (*Index* 2/1996, 1/1997, 6/1997, 1/1998, 2/1998, 3/1998). The court ruled that the original trial was flawed. (Reuters)

Chair of the Human Rights Association **Akin Birdal** (*Index* 4/1998), who survived an assassination attempt in May, was sentenced on 28 July, to one year in prison for 'provoking hatred'. The sentence came after a retrial following an appeal court's decision to overthrow a previous one-year sentence on the same charge. (Reuters, *Turkish Daily News*)

On 30 July **Cemal Dogan**, journalist for the daily *Sabah*, was the victim of an armed attack in front of his home in Ankara. The attack is thought to be connected to the publication of an article on extra-judicial executions. (RSF)

A number of prison officials were facing a formal inquiry on 30 July after allowing 70 Muslim sect members, accused of forming an illegal group, to wear Islamic dress in court. Aczimendis, with their long hair, monk-like robes and wailing ecstatic dances, often fall foul of dress codes dating back to reforms enacted in the 1920s by Ataturk. (Reuters)

On 30 July the trial of the editors of *Freedom of Thought Booklet 21* continued (*Index* 3/1998). Those volunteering as 'responsible editors' were journalist **Berat Guncukan**, musician **Sanar Yurdatapan**, journalist **Toktamys Ates** and publisher **Ugur Cankocak**. (Med-TV)

On 31 July journalist **Bisar Hazar** withdrew his candidacy for editor-in-chief of the bimonthly *Demokrat Baykan*, after he received death threats and pressure from the police and military. **Baris Goktekin, Cezmi Erdem, Keles Karasu, Seyitham Ari** and **Seyithan Yesilisik** had

resigned from the paper in June after continuous police harassment. The owner, **Erhan Palabayik**, had to leave the city where the paper is established following similar threats. (RSF)

On 31 July cartoonist **Dogan Guzel**, of the banned dailies *Ozgur Gundem* and *Ozgur Ulke*, was sentenced to three years' imprisonment for calling the state 'villain', through his cartoon character Kirik. He was charged with 'insulting the republic'. (RSF)

On the same day *Ulkede Gundem* journalist **Kerem Turk** was assaulted by police in front of the Palace of Justice in Urfa. After being asked to show his press credentials, he was attacked by plainclothes police. (RSF)

On 3 August eight writers were awarded Hellman/Hammett grants under the Human Rights Watch programme as writers who have suffered political persecution. Former *Yeni Yuzyil* journalist **Koray Duzgoren** has been repeatedly censored, fired and blacklisted for writing on Kurdish issues. The other seven names were withheld for safety reasons. (Human Rights Watch 3)

On 4 August playwright **Mehmet Vahi Yazar** was sentenced to 24 years in prison for *An Enemy of God*, which depicts the military as persecutors of devout Muslims. Four actors were also sentenced to 16 years. (Associated Press, BBC Online)

UKRAINE

On 29 June **Olexandre Syrtsov**, a reporter for the daily *Den*, was attacked on his way to work in Lviv. He was admitted to hospital with head and internal injuries after receiving numerous kicks to the head and torso. A specialist in politics, Syrtsov had written a number of articles critical of the local authorities. (RSF)

Finance Ministry inspectors announced on 1 July that approximately 10 million hryvnas (US$5 million) of clean-up funds allocated for the decontamination of the Chernobyl nuclear plant had been embezzled, misappropriated or misused. (RFE/RL)

UNITED KINGDOM

Both *The Sunday Times* and *News of the World* apologised to Virgin boss Richard Branson on 28 June. Branson has been subject to allegations of sexual harassment in the US. A statement agreed by lawyers indicated that Branson had not admitted that 'grabbing' had taken place, as previously suggested by the two newspapers. (*Guardian, The Sunday Times*)

A drum of diesel oil was thrown through the window of environmental campaigner **Colin Seymour** in East Yorkshire in early July. Seymour won a case against Flamborough parish counil in January 1997 which set a legal precedent. He prevented the destruction of a 50-metre strip of hedgerow. (*Guardian*)

• •

Legal wizardry

O n 14 November 1997, three editors of a British newspaper were each imprisoned for three years. On 23 July 1998 the Green Anarchist editors, or the Gandalf Three as they had become known, had their convictions quashed on appeal.

Their original trial judge had made plain that they were being jailed for what they had written, and the appeal judges found any calls upon a right to free expression an irrelevance. It seems the men were convicted and jailed in a land where the right to free speech means, in law, absolutely nothing. The release was granted on a technicality, as the excerpt from the judgement reproduced below makes clear; the trial judge and prosecution had confused the law relating to 'arson' and 'criminal damge'. The Gandalf Three are free now, but any right to free expression lies securely locked away. Their successful appeal, like their original trial, received virtually no press attention.

Lord Justice Henry:

'When the trial judge came to sum up the case he put the offence to the jury in the words of the indictment, ie: "To unlawfully incite persons unknown to commit criminal damage, contrary to Section 1(1) and (3) of the Criminal Damage Act, 1971. Conspiracy to incite persons unknown to commit criminal damage. Let us go to the far end of the chain that exists here. First, Criminal Damage. The aim of this alleged conspiracy is unlawfully to incite persons to commit criminal damage. A person commits criminal damage within the terms of this section if, without lawful excuse - and there is no suggestion that the people we are contemplating who might be involved in committing criminal damage would have any lawful excuse to do so: breaking butchers' shops windows, slashing the tires of vehicles: there is no suggestion of lawful excuse here. So it is criminal damage if a person, without lawful excuse, deliberately damages property belonging to another. That is very simple and it does not require any further definition from me."

It will be observed that in that passage the judge only directs them as to simple criminal damage. The examples he gives are of simple criminal damage. Nowhere in his summing-up does he give the jury any direction as to the separate offence of arson.

The likelihood must be that in a long trial, criminal damage was simply used as a catch all term for what was complained of, and no-one, not prosecution, not defence, and perhaps consequent on the first two, not the judge, realised that an offence contrary to Section 1(1) plus (3) of the Criminal Damage Act, 1971 could only refer to arson.' ❑

Frank Fisher & Emily Mitchell

• •

On 29 July Home Secretary Jack Straw revealed that the domestic intelligence service MI5 had amassed files on nearly 500,000 people since its inception in 1909. The files will not be made available to the public. (*Guardian, Times*)

USA

On 15 June District Court Judge Audrey Collins struck down a key part of the 1966 Anti-Terrorism and Effective Death Penalty law when he ruled, on free speech grounds, that it was legal for the Liberation Tigers of Tamil Eelam (LTTE), the Kurdistan Workers Party (PKK) and other groups designated as 'terrorist' by the federal government last October to receive training in the country for 'lawful pursuits'. (Reuters)

A week after a federal judge had stripped him of his First Amendment defence and a week before going to trial, National Public Radio reporter Larry Matthews was forced to plead guilty on 6 July to one count of receiving pornographic images online and one count of transmitting child pornography. Matthews maintains that the material seized by the FBI from his home computer two years ago was for research into a story. He faces up to 15 years in prison and US$250,000 (£150,000) for each count. By pleading guilty, Matthews will be able to petition the Court of Appeals more quickly than if he had gone to trial. (Associated Press, *Wired*)

James Fallows was dismissed as editor of the third-ranking news magazine *US News & World Report* on 6 July, following disagreements with owner Mortimer Zuckerman over the slashing of the editorial budget and the latter's push for more rehash of the previous week's news. Three staffers claim that Fallows also fought Zuckerman's attempt to assign a story on Hispanic culture to Bianca Jagger, whom he had once dated. (*International Herald Tribune*)

A First Amendmentt challenge of the government's encryption export regulations was rejected by an Ohio District Court on 2 July because of the judge's opinion that 'cryptographic source code is not speech'. This contradicts last August's California ruling that cryptography export controls violate First Amendment rights, and could mark the beginning of cryptography's journey to the Supreme Court. On 7 July, White House Commerce Secretary William Daley said software companies would be permitted to sell encryption software to powerful financial institutions in 45 countries abroad, but not Russia, China or Mexico. (*Wired*)

Dateline NBC was ordered in early July to pay $525,000 (£310,000) in damages to a trucking company because of 'negligent reporting' in a segement on safety violations by truckers. The federal court case in Bangor, Maine, did not focus on whether or not the 1995 report was true, but whether the NBC journalists 'misrepresented the slant of the story' to those they had interviewed. One interviewee, trucker Peter Kennedy, admitted to driving almost halfway across the US without sleep. (*International Herald Tribune*)

A defendant in a Los Angeles court was given a 50,000-volt shock over eight seconds for speaking out of turn. **Ronald Hawkins** was defending himself at a sentencing hearing when judge Joan Comparet-Cassani ordered a bailiff to activate the REACT belt fitted on him because of past incidents when Hawkins had acted violently. The judge twice warned Hawkins not to interrupt her and, when he persisted, she gave the order. Hawkins' last utterance before the power surged through his body was 'that is unconstitutional'.(Reuters)

UZBEKISTAN

On 28 June **Shadi Mardiev**, a reporter with the state-run Samarkand radio station, was sentenced to 11 years in prison for defamation and extortion. Mardiev is known for his satirical writings in the journal *Mushtum*. The suit against him stemmed from a broadcast which satirised the corrupt practices of the Samarkand deputy prosecutor Talat Abdulkhalikzada, who alleged that Mardiev attempted to use the broadcast to extort money from him. Mardiev, who was arrested last November and detained until his court date in June, suffered two brain haemorrhages in detention and remains in solitary confinement. (CPJ, WAN,

•••••••••••••••••••••••••••••••••

Martín Espada

Wretched of the Earth

D^{ear Index,}

I am writing to you with news of Mumia Abu-Jamal, and a new poem of mine. As you know I wrote the poem for Mumia called 'Another Nameless Prostitute Says the Man is Innocent',which National Public Radio (NPR) censored and which was published in your journal (*Index 5/1997*).

I visited Mumia in prison at the beginning of May. Since I am a lawyer, I gained access to the prison as a legal visitor. Journalists and their audio/video equipment are barred from this and other Pennsylvania prisons (a prohibition informally known as 'the Mumia Rule').

The State Correctional Institution-Greene has been the scene of savage repression in the last two years. The *Pittsburgh Post-Gazette* reported one incident where an inmate named Antonio Noguerol was severely beaten, then watched as a 'guard dipped a finger into the blood and traced the letters 'KKK' on the blood-stained floor. Noticing a gold tooth in Noguerol's mouth, the guard jammed his night-stick into the inmate's mouth and knocked out the tooth.' More than 200 lawsuits have been filed against the prison.

Many of these inmates turned to Mumia, as a well-known jailhouse lawyer and journalist, for advice on law or the media.

Recently, the Department of Corrections found a unique way to retaliate against him and others like him. A new rule was established, requiring that all personal property of inmates must be kept in a single box, 12 by 12 by 14 inches. One day, four guards entered Mumia's cell and confiscated 17 boxes of books and legal documents. He could send these boxes home, if he could afford to, but he could not keep them. His library was gone. The inmates staged two hunger strikes in response to this and other rulings.

When I saw Mumia, he said: 'I would rather be beaten than have this assault on the life of the mind.' He told me he chose to keep *Beloved* in the box. Then he said 'Giving up a book is like giving up a child, like parting with your own flesh. How do you choose between *Beloved* and *The Wretched of the Earth?*'

Then his eyes welled up, and a single tear ran down his face. At the same moment, I could see, in the Plexiglas separating us, the reflection of the guards outside the visiting room, walking across Mumia's forehead. The next day I wrote a poem on the experience.

The poem, I think, is relevant to a journal concerned with freedom of expression. Mumia is a political prisoner. Robert Meeropol, the younger son of Julius and Ethel Rosenberg, maintains that Mumia is the first political prisoner in the US to face the death penalty since the Rosenbergs. Mumia is an important journalist, essayist and intellectual, yet he has been crudely censored by the mainstream media (ie NPR).

The prison system has also censored him in many ways, from the 'Mumia Rule' to solitary confinement as punishment for 'engaging in the profession of journalism'. Now they have taken his books away. Mumia has recently enrolled in an advanced degree

•••••••••••••••••••••••••••••••••

programme. He wondered how he will complete that degree without books.

The poem is a documentary, a dispatch from a place where the camera and the tape recorder are forbidden. I wrote that dispatch in verse simply because I am a poet and not a journalist. Whatever its artistic character, there are also compelling journalistic and political reasons for the existence of the poem, and for sending the poem to Index.

This is not a censored poem. However, it is a poem about a censored, incarcerated writer and thinker. It is a sequel to the first Mumia poem, providing an update on his condition and a more intimate view of that condition.

There is some urgency here: the ruling on Mumia's appeal to the Pennsylvania Supreme Court is now due, and his enemies have recently published ads at great expense in the New York Times and elsewhere to condemn him. Mumia's attorneys feel that the disposition of the state court may well be unfavourable and many observers believe that the timing of the judgment may have been influenced by the presence on campus of the students who have been among his staunchest defenders, now on summer vacation. Thank you for your consideration.

Sincerely
Martín Espada ❏

[*As a result of the two hunger strikes described above, SCI-Greene prisoners are now permitted a second 12x12x14 inch box in which to store their personal possessions. There are presently more than 100 prisoners on SCI-Greene's Death Row.*]

Prisoner AM-8335 and his Library of Lions

For Mumia Abu-Jamal, SCI-Greene, Waynesburg, PA

When the guards handcuffed inmates in the shower
and shoved them skidding naked to concrete,
or the blue shirts billyclubbed a prisoner
to wrench the gold from his jaw,
to swirl KKK in his spat blood,
the numbered men pressed their fingertips
against the smooth cool pages of your voice,
that voice of many books,
and together you whispered in the yard
about lawsuits, about the newspapers.

From the battlements
the warden trumpeted a proclamation:
in every cell one box per inmate,
twelve by twelve by fourteen,
for all personal possessions. You say
four blue shirts crowded your death row cell
to wrestle seventeen cartons away,
wrinkled paperbacks in pillars

● ●

toppling, history or law collected and studied
like the bones of a fossilised predator,
a library beyond Carnegie's whitest visions of marble.
One guard would fondle a book
emblazoned with the word *Revolutionary*, muttering:
This is what we're supposed to get.

Today, after the hunger strike,
you sit windowed in the visiting room,
prisoner AM-8335: dreadlocks blooming
like an undiscovered plant of the rain forest,
hands coupled in the steel cuffs,
brown skin against the striped prison jump-suit,
tapestry of the chain gang.

I would rather be beaten, you say,
than this assault on the life of the mind.
You keep Toni Morrison's book in your box with the toothpaste.
You gaze through the glass at the towering apparition
of your library, as if climbing marble steps.

As you say:
Giving up a book is like giving up a child,
like parting with your own flesh.
How do you choose between *Beloved* and *The Wretched of the Earth*?

Your eyes pool.
A single tear is the scarification of your cheekbone,
a warrior's ceremonial gash on death row.
Across the glass a reflection of the guards walking,
small blue men patrolling your forehead.

In the parking lot, I turn again towards the prison,
walls ribboned with jagged silver loops of wire,
and see a great library
with statues of lions at the gate. ❏

Martín Espada *is the author of five poetry collections, including* Imagine the Angels of Bread *(WW Norton), which won the Before Columbus Foundation's American Book Award.*

● ●

Glasnost Defence Foundation)

VATICAN

In early July the Pope issued an apostolic letter, To Defend Faith, aimed at eliminating dissent over issues such as the ordination of women, abortion and euthanasia. In an explanatory note, Cardinal Joseph Ratzinger insisted that 'every believer is required to give firm and definitive assent' to 'truths'. The ruling is particularly aimed at those who teach the faith and failure to comply may result in excommunication. (*Guardian, International Herald Tribune*)

VENEZUELA

Presidential candidate **Irene Sáez** made public on 4 June that she had received death threats during the past December presidential elections in the form of telephone calls and e-mail messages. The former Miss Universe came second in the polls. (*Latin American Press*)

On 5 June the lawyer and human rights activist **Carlos Bieta Palma** was illegally detained and intimidated for a few hours as he was leaving his office. He was warned to be careful of 'what he became involved in'. (The Observatory, The Human Rights Action Network)

YEMEN

On 8 July, an 'official source' warned the media against presenting news of the country and its development in an 'improper way' using 'falsehoods and exaggerations'. Correspondents, news agencies and satellite channels were threatened with court action should they indulge in such reporting. (*Al-Hayat*)

ZAMBIA

On 13 June government official accused unnamed private newspapers of having a hidden agenda to discredit the ruling Movement for Multi-party Democracy leadership and warned that the party is running out of patience with the publications for 'perpetuating insults against President Frederick Chiluba' and other leaders. The independent *Post* newspaper recently published a story exposing Mulenga's alleged extramarital affair. (MISA)

ZIMBABWE

President Robert Mugabe hinted on 13 July that his government will introduce laws to monitor freedom of the press in his country, saying there had been tendencies to 'manufacture lies' in some sections of the press and that he would not allow this to continue. (PANA)

The government's virtual monopoly of the mass media has allowed it to censor information about growing popular opposition, Article 19 said in a report published on 10 June. The report lists how the authorities deny freedom of expression by hiring and firing editorial staff, and issuing directives to newsrooms. (A19)

Recent publications: *Media Monopoly and Popular Protest* (A19, June 1998, pp 28)

Compiled by: *Lucy Hillier, Regina Jere-Malanda (Africa); Peter Beveridge, Andrew Kendle, Jennie Roberts, Nicky Winstanley-Torode (Asia); Simon Martin, Vera Rich (eastern Europe and CIS); Dolores Cortes (south and central America); Rupert Clayton, Gill Newsham, M. Siraj Sait (Middle East); Andrew Elkin, Suzanne Fisher (north America and Pacific); Andrew Blick (UK and western Europe).*

NITA YIN YIN MAY

Under the dragon

Ten years ago, after a series of bloody confrontations in which up to 5,000 Burmese were killed by security forces – more than in the 1989 Tiananmen massacre – the Burmese military took over the government of the country in September 1988 and instituted severe censorship with total disregard for human rights. Despite the overwhelming victory of the National League for Democracy in the 1990 elections, the military remains in power. Burma's economy is in ruins and human rights abuses continue; but the generals show no willingness for dialogue and, as the anniversary of their takeover approached, renewed their attacks on the NLD and its leader, Aung San Suu Kyi

Ten years have passed since it all happened – 1988 to 1998. For some people 10 years is forever; for others 10 years seems a moment ago. To me, what happened 10 years ago seems as if it happened yesterday.

I can still remember that silence, that strange kind of silence – one that I have never experienced in my life – a kind of silence that I feared and dreaded – and hope that I will never hear again.

The smell of dried and rotting blood comes back to me together with the scent of dried and rotting flowers left behind by the loved ones and mourners. A solitary monk's umbrella lay on the ground, too. A small crowd of people milled around totally and completely devoid of speech unable to offer any kind of hope or consolation to each other. The only sound that broke the silence was the roar of military trucks.

This was the scene that came flashing back to me as I read *Under the Dragon*. This was the scene in front of the Rangoon General Hospital. The doctors and nurses came out from the wards to request the troops not to shoot the wounded and to save the lives of those that were dying, but got themselves shot in the act of saving others.

Even now, I can still hear the voice of a student, shouting on the phone, 'Come and get us – come and get us – we're trapped and students all around me are wounded and they're still shooting from all angles.' But to my shame I wasn't able to go to them. Circumstances prevented me from doing so. That was on 18 September 1988.

I received three more similar calls that very day from different locations in the downtown area. I have never, never felt so helpless in my life. I often hear these voices and I wonder whether they're still alive, or if they're in jail, or perhaps are free and doing well.

I remember banging my head repeatedly against the wall and on the desk at the British Embassy where I worked. I hope these students will forgive me for letting them down. I was so angry and frustrated with my helplessness. Then I came to my senses: of course, I was nothing; I couldn't give any kind of assistance. How could I in such a time, when hell seemed to have broken loose. Each time the phone rang it was a desperate cry for help. It was not only I who was unable to help; even the Red Cross couldn't help, for they were also being fired at. I myself had fled the scene of shooting many times, but the only thing I lost were my slippers. Some of those students lost their lives, some their future.

Let me tell you about the time that I lost. While I was in prison, I wasn't allowed to read or write and my precious time was stolen from me. I had despaired that I would ever get it back. That is why I have now set aside one hour from my daily sleeping time to make up for the lost time. I lost a total of 13,080 hours while in prison, so it will take me some nine years to make it up. As I was released in 1992, I'll not be getting back my lost hours until 2001.

The scars have never healed, and although time has passed, what we suffered cannot be forgotten. It is like a disease without a cure, without a remedy, and time has not lived up to its name as a healer so far. And I feel, somehow, that the world has forgotten the plight of the Burmese people. It's not enough remembering and commemorating anniversaries. Something should be done and I hope *Under the Dragon* will help in the search for a cure, just as John Pilger's *Inside Burma: Land of Fear* has done and many other articles, videos and films on Burma. ❏

Nita Yin Yin May was a writer and publisher in Burma. She was arrested and imprisoned under Burma's censorship laws. She now lives in London

The ruined temples of Pagan, Burma – Credit: Rex

RORY MACCLEAN

Love in a hot climate

Prostitution does not exist in Burma; at least it cannot be mentioned in the press. The Burmese kings had a history of taking numerous wives, and religious sites always offered the services of 'pagoda servants' to pilgrims. Neither custom still exists today, officially. The girls on the steps of pagodas sell flowers and candles, religious requisites, not physical comforts. The royal *zenana* has been replaced by the executive escort agency. But both traditions remain part of the culture and, as a result of the smallest misfortune, a woman can become trapped.

Louis' dollars, though worth a fortune to Ni Ni, didn't last until the end of the monsoon. Soon after her return to Waybagi she fell ill, and May May Gyi spent the money on medicines which did nothing to improve her condition. No drug seemed capable of restoring her energy, no tonic would lift her spirit. Buddhists are taught that they are responsible today for what they will be tomorrow. Every man and woman is answerable for their own actions. But Ni Ni's sense of duty had left with Louis' departing aeroplane. The roar of its engines had shaken the satellite town. Like her father before her she brooded through the airless, vaporous afternoons, not hearing the rain drumming on her roof, ignoring May May Gyi's encouragement, even turning down Law San's offer of *Shan hkauk-hswe* noodles. The past was memory, the future might only be fantasy, but she had no love in the here and now. Ni Ni did not feel anger, wished no vengeance, and when the money ran out, when there seemed to be no other choice, she went in search of Way Way.

Way Way's friend promised to find her work in Thailand as a dishwasher. The wage he promised was double that which she could earn in Rangoon. He paid for her bus ticket to the border, where she was met by a Thai driver. There were five other women in her car: two Burmese, two Shan girls with milky-white complexions and a single, silent Chinese. On the road to Bangkok the driver paid a uniformed man at a checkpoint. In the brothel Ni Ni was given a number and told to sit in a windowed showroom. She toyed with the hem of her blouse when bypassers stopped to stare at her. The first man who took her in the *hong bud oree sut*, 'the room to unveil virgins', paid the owner 120 *baht* – less than five dollars – and tipped her the same amount. During that month she was sold as a virgin to four more clients. She was allowed to keep her tips. They were the largest she was to receive over the next four years.

The friend had been an agent. The debt which enslaved Ni Ni was his fee, plus her transport, clothes and protection money, compounded by 100 per cent interest. She was required to wear high heels and a mini-skirt instead of her silk *longyi*. In lieu of money she received red plastic chips; one for every client. Each morning she counted them twice to calcutate the amount that had been subtracted from her debt. She kept them under the cement bunk on which she was forced to prostitute herself. Under it also was the secret door to a locker where she hid during police raids. The abrupt arrival of a dozen armed officers never failed to alarm the brothel owner. More often, though, the policemen came in ones and twos after work. However they arrived, the girls were always theirs for free.

The cubicle measuring six feet square was her home. Here Ni Ni slept and worked, twelve hours a day, seven days a week. Only two days a month were allowed off, during her period. The clients were mostly Asian, although westerners paid for her too, flying in from Frankfurt and Brussels on 'sex bomber' package holidays. She served five or six men each weekday. On weekends she often had as many as thirty customers.

The demand for new faces dictated that every few months she be moved to a different brothel. Each was the same as the last. The neon-lit rooms were dingy, the walls always stained grimy grey along the edge of the bunk. There were never any proper toilets. Once, in one cubicle she though she heard the sea, though it could have been a passing *tuk-tuk*, and from another, if she stood on the bed and peered through a grille, she could make out the graceful spires of the Royal Palace. The frequent displacement left her no time to get to know the other girls or to consider escape, especially as she never knew where she was incarcerated. Those who did run away were often caught by their police clients and returned to be punished, or locked up for months without trial, subjected to abuse, in a Thai immigration detention centre. The few who managed to reach Burma risked the possibility of arrest for 'illegal departure', and even, it was rumoured, execution if they were found to be HIV positive. Their only choice was to work until they were told their debt was paid, then to rely on an agent to escort them back through the checkpoints and over the border.

The years crept up on her, ageing Ni Ni's firm young body. Men chose her less often, and those who did were less particular. One client put a gun to her head when she asked him to wear a condom. It wasn't because she was afraid of pregnancy – she had often paid the owner's wife to give her Depo-Prevera injections – or even because he was filthy. It was simply that he frightened her. In life there is a path of fear and a path of love, and Ni Ni had been unable to follow the latter one alone.

The owner threatened her with a beating if she ever came out of the
room before her client again.

Ni Ni's hands touched and stroked and satisfied the men, but she felt
nothing, sensed nothing through the empty years. Only sometimes, in
an Englishman's clumsy white embrace, did she remember Louis. But he
never came to rescue her. At eighteen she was over-handled and utterly
misused. Her life had been stolen. She had lost control of her body. She
possessed nothing more than a sense of hopelessness.

It is estimated that two million people are employed in Thailand's sex
trade. The business is probably the most valuable sector of the tourist
industry, which itself exceeds all exports as a source of foreign exchange.
In 1988, 4.3 million people visited the country, three-quarters of whom
were unaccompanied males. But it is local patronage that makes the
greater demand. Half of all Thai men have their first sexual experience
with a prostitute; three out of four have visited a brothel. The majority
of commercial sex workers are natives, but there are also Filipinas,
Indonesians, even Europeans – five thousand Russian prostitutes are
working in Bangkok. And every year, ten thousand Burmese women,
young and infection-free, are trafficked across the border, enticed by false
promises, imprisoned by debt bondage. Their great hope is to go home,
but their greater fear is deportation.

Often, in the quiet of morning, when Ni Ni was left alone, she fell
into the same dream. In her cubicle a miniature black spider, no bigger
than a pinhead, crawled up her hand. She watched it spin between her
thumb and forefinger a silky thread which glistened and grew until it
twisted together her five fingers. She felt its tickle as both her hands were
enmeshed. The bonds became tighter and she tried to free herself. But
the industrious spider, so friendly and engaging at first, continued its
labours, stitched its weave, wrapped the corners, until all her body, the
bunk on which she lay, even the red plastic chips were wrapped in its
cobweb, dusty and dirty, and her life was snuffed out.

It was from this dream that Ni Ni was awoken by the sound of
English voices. The central Crime Suppression Division – in
cooperation with the Commission for the Protection of Children's
Rights – raided her hotel in an operation stage-managed for the world's
press. The girls were arrested and interrogated for the cameras, though
they were not asked question about the brothel owner. He had been
allowed to go, along with the pimps and the clients. Ni Ni and the other

Burmese nationals were sent to the penal reform institution in Pakkret, from where they were deported. In that brief period when Rangoon sanctioned repatriation, no brothel agents nor Thai border patrol officers could lure the women back to Bangkok's red light districts. They were not harassed in local jails or raped in reform houses. There was no need for them to buy their release papers. The Shan and hill-tribe prostitutes, not being ethnic Burmans, were less fortunate. The Burmese authorities forbade their return because they were members of a tribal minority. They, like the fresh-faced girls who arrived every morning at Bangkok's Northern Bus Terminal, were left to their fates in Thailand.

On the flight home, Ni Ni caught sight of golden Shwedagon. She watched the red earth of Rangoon rush up to meet the aircraft. She saw the delta-winged shadow flash over the dusty plain. She was taken to the North Okkalapa Female Police Training Academy. A doctor tested her blood. There were injections and tablets to be taken every day. The girls were told that they could go home as soon as their parents came to collect them. Some families were too poor to travel to the capital. There was no one to claim Ni Ni, and almost a year passed before she was released from the barracks.

★★★★★

Pagan has not remained uninhabited since the days of the Mongols. Earlier in the twentieth century, farmers returned to settle among the *kyaung* ruins. A village had developed and, during my first visit to Burma, I had eaten in a family restaurant and stayed up until dawn watching a local *pwe* festival. But from our peaceful, idyllic eyrie Katrin and I spotted no sign of the marketplace or tumbledown food stalls. There were no bamboo houses, villagers or school, only new hotels and sightseeing guides. The site had been transformed into a museum for tourists.

On the ride back to our hotel, I asked Soe Htun what had happened to the old village. 'Kublai Khan destroy,' he replied. 'Rape and pillage all of old Pagan. Very bad man.'

'No, more recently than that,' I said. 'Maybe last year? Two years ago?' Soe Htun turned to stare at me and I thought for a moment that he hadn't understood. 'There was a town here when I last visited.'

'No town, no sir,' he replied, fidgeting with the reins. A furtiveness had crept into his behaviour. 'A few farmers, maybe, but no town.'

'Ten years ago I stayed at a place called the Mother Hotel. And I remember a sign at a restaurant which said, "Be kind to animals by not eating them".'

The cart turned from the track and onto a new tarmac carriageway. A gust of wind from a passing tour bus filled with Taiwanese holidaymakers almost blew us off the road. For a moment the only sound was the clip-clop of hooves on the tarmac. 'Today is my first day as horse-cart driver,' Soe Htun said. 'My grandfather buy for me. It is our business, you understand.'

'We wish you success,' said Katrin.

'It must be success,' he insisted. 'You see I hoping many tourists come to Pagan so one day I can buy a cart for myself.' It seemed unlikely; the horse and cart would have cost Soe Htun's grandfather the equivalent of two years' salary. He would also have had to bribe local officials to secure one of the 150 tourist horse cart licences. 'My grandfather take 30 per cent of my daily money so not leave much for saving, but one day I will make prosperous.' He took a breath. 'That is why it is important not to talk about some things.'

There was no further mention of the missing village. As the cart passed under an avenue of tamarind trees, Soe Htun asked us if we wanted to go swimming at the Thiripyitsaya Hotel. It seemed that the pool was open to non-residents, of the hotel and the country, but the thought did not appeal. We were tired from our travels and I paid him. 'The first money that I earn,' he said, slapping the notes on the cart and on the horse itself. 'They bring me luck. It is my good fortune that you have come to Pagan. Please, sir, tomorrow we go to buy souvenirs?' ❑

From Under the Dragon: Travels in Burma *by* **Rory MacClean**
(HarperCollins, 3rd August 1998, £16.99)

JUDITH VIDAL-HALL

Ulysses' journey

In addition to the reams of rejection slips that marked his relationship with the publishers – and printers who refused persistently to set type – of Great Britain, James Joyce, acknowledged even in his own life as one of the most important writers of the century, also fought an uncompromising and lifelong battle with the censors throughout the Anglo-Saxon world. Few of his books were trouble free, but it was *Ulysses*, that 'world disturbing sailor', as Joyce called it, that focused the wrath of the moralists and exercised even the most ardent of its literary supporters.

When *Ulysses* did finally appear, in March 1918, serialised in a small US literary journal, *The Little Review*, it unleashed a storm of abuse: the 'outraged' and 'disgusted' of bourgeois America were, alas, not rendered speechless. According to the *Review*'s founding editor, Margaret Anderson, the following is a typical reaction:

> 'I think this is the most damnable slush and filth that ever polluted paper in print ... There are no words I know to describe, even vaguely, how disgusted I am; not with the mire of his effusion but with all those whose minds are so putrid that they dare allow such muck and sewage of the human mind to besmirch the world by repeating it – and in print, through which medium it may reach young minds. Oh my God, the horror of it.'

Over the next decade or so, Anderson and *Ulysses* were subjected to a good deal more in similar vein.

But *Ulysses* offended more than vice crusaders and government officials such as those in the US Post Office, who were the first officially to suppress Joyce's masterpiece by refusing it access to the mails on the grounds that it was 'obscene, lewd or lascivious' within the meaning of the US Criminal Code. D H Lawrence – ironically, *Lady Chatterley's Lover* was cited together with *Ulysses* on a 1931 post office seizure form – called the 'Penelope' episode 'the dirtiest, most indecent, obscene thing ever written'; Virginia Woolf dismissed it as 'merely the scratchings of pimples on the body of the bootboy' (Joyce himself she described as 'a virile he-goat'). And the first 'censor' of *Ulysses* was none other than its foremost champion, Ezra Pound, then foreign editor of *The Little Review*. Before sending Joyce's typescript of the Calypso episode to *TLR*, he excised passages he thought most likely and most instantly to provoke government authorities. Among them he tells Joyce in a letter defending his decision, were 'about twenty lines' from the 'jakes' passage describing Bloom's early morning defecations. Pound also had trouble with the presence of 'urine' in the opening of the episode but let it go, exercising his prerogative as editor on a later passage describing Bloom's thoughts as he makes his way home carrying the kidney he will eat for breakfast and reflecting on an advertisement that has conjured up visions of the exotic eastern Mediterranean life. Then a cloud passes on the horizon, casting a pall on his thoughts.

> 'No, not like that. A barren land, bare waste. Vulcanic lake, the dead sea: no fish, weedless, sunk deep in the earth. No wind could lift those waves, grey metal, poisonous foggy waters. Brimstone they called it raining down: the cities of the plain: Sodom, Gommorah, Edom All dead names. A dead sea in a dead land, grey and old. Old now. It bore the oldest, the first race. A bent hag crossed from Cassidy's, clutching a naggin bottle by the neck. The oldest people. Wandering far away over all the earth, multiplying, dying, being born everything. It lay there now. Now it could bear no more. Dead: an old woman's: the grey sunken [cunt] of the world.'

Pound had his reasons and 'cunt' became 'belly' in *TLR*. His primary concern was to get the work published. He may also, Paul Vanderham, author of *James Joyce and Censorship*, claims, have had more personal reasons for his deletions, ones that were at variance with the practical and aesthetic considerations he expounded to Joyce in the letter explaining his decisions.

Ulysses broke a long list of taboos still operating in the twilight world of a lingering nineteenth century morality – not all of them by any means vanished on the eve of the twenty-first. Ridicule and denigration of royalty, masturbation, 'detailed treatment of dropping faeces', graphic accounts of the sex act, blasphemy and the constant confounding of the erotic and the scatological. Even its style was threatening and subversive:

Joyce groupies on the Ulysses trail,

'literary bolshevism' said one critic, fearing its incitement to revolution in the agitated post-war political climate of the USA in early 1919.

Ulysses' seizure by US customs officials, a 13-year ban on its distribution and a series of obscenity trials that lasted from 1920-1934 had, claims Vanderham, a profound effect not only on the structure and writing of *Ulysses* itself, but radically altered the style of subsequent books. Well before the troublesome sailor was safely in harbour in the Anglo-Saxon world, *Finnegan's Wake*, Joyce's last book, was appearing in serial form in the French periodical *transition*. Joyce claimed finally to have evolved a style he claimed was 'censor proof': of all his work, *Finnegan's Wake* was virtually alone in escaping the interest of the censor. He had succeeded, finally, in making 'obscenity safe for literature'. But not, as Vanderham implies, at the cost either of self-censorship or compromise. Was not this simply a matter of stylistic evolution natural in a writer constantly challenging the literary as well as the social modes of his day?

So far so good and not so remarkable. Vanderham now launches into a novel, and not entirely persuasive, thesis. The famous 1934 judgement that released *Ulysses* from its trials in the USA and prepared the way for its liberation elsewhere – Ireland lifted its exclusion order later the same year, Britain followed suit in 1936; Australia, which lifted the ban in 1937, lowered it again in 1941; it took Canada until 1949 to give it passage – was, he claims, based on 'well-intentioned lies', concocted by Joyce's admirers and allowed by a well disposed judge.

Briefly: to get *Ulysses* off the hook, Judge Woolsey allowed the 'well intentioned lies' of the book's defenders to construct an aesthetic theory of art that argues that good literature cannot, by its very excellence as high art, corrupt or be obscene. They removed literature and art from any connection with the land of the living. Woolsey's judgement determined that a genuine work of literature can have no harmful effect, whether moral, political or religious, on the beliefs and actions of its readers. Therein, argues Vanderham, 'rests their misrepresentation of the proper basis for freedom of speech'. By appealing to this 'aesthetic' view of art, the basis for such freedom becomes the idea that art 'affects nothing, subverts nothing, strengthens nothing'. Not, one feels, a view that would comfort the novelists and poets of the Soviet Union – or Latin America, Africa, China and all too many parts of the globe – who found themselves dead, disappeared or in the gulag as a result of their fictions. But, equally, not one that bears the opprobrium cast on by Vanderham. It did, after all, achieve its objective. And continues to serve in contemporary censorship debates; as in the controversy surrounding *The Satanic Verses* for instance.

But this the author of *James Joyce and Censorship* will not allow. What then must we do? In true libertarian fashion and with a conviction that only those living in the land of the First Amendment can assume, Vanderham ends with a passionate plea for the only 'lasting foundation for freedom of speech':

> 'Ultimately, a lasting commitment to freedom of speech can be based only on respect for the individual's need to express himself or herself freely, and recognition that such respect is essential to the common good. Far from denying that people are influenced by what they read, such respect must openly acknowledge that even works we refuse to censor may be harmful in certain respects. Rooted as it is in respect for the dignity of the human person and recognition of the common good, this view affirms that our commitment to freedom of speech will necessarily require suffering on our part, but that it is better to let the weeds grow with the wheat than to destroy the wheat to get rid of the weeds.'

Yes indeed. But we do not all live in the land of the free; nor do we have the luxury of choosing our defence. The well intentioned defence constructed in the very different climate of the 1920s was a skillful – and successful – evasion of prevailing prejudices rather than the 'lie' Vanderham's intransigent and at times hysterical absolutism would have it. ❏

Paul Vanderham, James Joyce and Censorship: The Trials of Ulysses *(New York University Press, August 1998, £45)*

SARAH A SMITH

Breaking the code

A 'grossly immoral woman', a lesbian icon, a self-styled congenital invert. Novelist Radclyffe Hall has always been a controversial figure. Early this year the Home Office added to her notoriety when it decided some of the documents relating to Hall's 1928 trial for obscenity still constituted a threat to national security and would not be included among the papers released into the public domain in January this year.

Already aware of much of the substance of the case from the notes, letters and transcripts of the proceedings kept by Hall and her solicitor Harold Rubinstein, Diana Souhami, author of a new biography, *The Trials of Radclyffe Hall*, discovered this latest episode in what Hall herself called a 'conspiracy of silence' against her pioneering lesbian novel, *The Well of Loneliness*, when she went in search of details of how law makers and enforcers had connived against Hall and her 'disgusting' book 70 years earlier.

While the newly released documents including unsuspected evidence of the continuation of the ban under the ostensibly more liberal government of Clement Attlee in 1946, many files were empty and marked 'Retained by the Home Office'. Souhami was told that the decision to hold some papers back had been made 'in the interests of national security'. The documents would not be considered for release again until 2007.

Only after she took the matter to Home Secretary Jack Straw's office did Souhami gain access to the records in their entirety. The suppressed papers added, she says, 'more pieces to the jigsaw'. The extent of Stanley Baldwin's government's bigotry was already clear, as was the determination of Home Secretary Sir William Joynson-Hicks, Director of Public Prosecutions Sir Archibald Bodkin, and Attorney General Sir Thomas Inskip to secure a ban. But the issuing of warrants requiring the Post Office to intercept mail addressed to the book's Paris publisher, the schemes to indict London publisher Jonathan Cape and distributor

Radclyffe Hall and Una Troubridge, 1927 - Credit: Weidenfeld & Nicolson

Leopold Hill, not to mention the circumnavigating of the Chairman of the Board of Customs (who refused to take part in the case against *The Well*), were the sort of 'details' Souhami was after.

Her biography is undoubtedly enriched by the trial papers from which she quotes extensively. It is her trial and treatment by the male establishment that make Hall and *The Well of Loneliness* – the only one of her seven extant novels that excited controversy – significant.

The Well was Hall's fifth book and she told her publisher Jonathan Cape: 'I wrote it out of a deep sense of duty. I am proud to have taken up the pen in defence of those who are utterly defenceless.' A melodramatic and convoluted tale of lesbian anguish, it is a book about martyrdom rather than pleasure. Rose Macauley suggested that far from depraving anyone, it would probably have 'a salutary effect'.

It was tried, however, on the basis of its lesbian theme rather than any educative impact and it was not tried fairly. Trial by jury was avoided out of fear a jury would be swayed by an articulate defence. In spite of the experts both defence and prosecution amassed, only one witness, a policeman, was admitted. The chief magistrate, Sir Chartres Biron, was the embodiment of the law, his opinion indisputable. And his opinion, and that of the appeal judge, Sir Robert Wallace, was that *The Well* was 'corrupting in its tendency, a condonation of unnatural practices and prejudicial to the morals of the community'.

But the most pernicious thing, says Souhami, was the silence, the lack of any discussion. Hall had the courage to break the silence surrounding lesbian relations, says her biographer. 'All the Bloomsbury lot were having homosexual relationships and writing about them in coded terms.' Hall was blunter; she changed the pronouns. In many ways, *The Well* is rather a naive book and could and should have paved the way for others. Censorship ensured there wouldn't be any others.'

It also ensured huge sales for the book which continued to be printed in Paris throughout the British ban, lifted only in 1949 and was a great success in the USA where a trial for obscenity in 1929 failed. Today, *The Well* enjoys cult status, ranking eleventh in Virago's Modern Classics best-seller list.

Drawing on Hall's unpublished papers, and the letters and diaries of the author and her three great loves, society beauty Mabel Batten, an Admiral's wife Una Lady Troubridge and Russian emigré Evguenia Souline, Souhami spares the reader no detail of their high life and low prejudices – Hall and Una were fervent fans of Mussolini – and the battles waged in the name of love: especially the battles.

It is hard to square Souhami's portrait of a sexually domineering patriarch with the writer of the dour *The Well*. Far from living the largely monastic life of her heroine Stephen Gordon, Hall was something of a rake. She used sex as a weapon, first against her much-hated mother

(her early lovers seem to have been chosen from among her mother's relatives) and then as a brand of possession, writing in a panic to the unfortunate Souline: 'You belong to me, and don't you forget it. No-one but me has the right to touch you. I took your virginity, do you hear?'

Among the stylish lesbians of Hall's acquaintance were Tallulah Bankhead, Colette, Romaine Brooks and Natalie Barney, none of whom fitted Hall's definition of 'some of the most persecuted and misunderstood people in the world'. One senses a restrained mockery in Souhami's approach, an antidote to Hall's extraordinarily inflated idea of her own importance as an 'artistic brain-worker' and member of the moneyed elite.

But for all the humour she brings to her description of Hall's interest in the paranormal after Batten's death, the battles with the local church in Rye and the endless problems with substandard pets, Souhami writes with appalled sympathy on the subject of Hall's 'trials'. These weren't just legal. The last 10 years of Hall's life were spent in what Souhami calls 'sheer hell', albeit a self-imposed one. Tired of her 'wife' Una but psychologically dependent upon her, Hall tried to engineer a menage à trois with her and Souline. It was not an arrangement any of them could stomach and, after years of struggle and debilitating depression, Hall died cut off from Souline by the increasingly manipulative Una.

Hall saw herself as a role model for 'inverts' and her life is certainly more exciting than her fiction. But the idea of using either as a template is problematic. Hall was too much of her class to see very far beyond it and was not, frankly, interested in anybody else's rights but her own. Una supported the suppression of books in fascist Italy: libertarian they were not.

Today it is possible to publish fiction much more direct than *The Well of Loneliness* and to live free of the curious stares that its 'freakish' hero inspired. But silence still afflicts lesbians in public life and, except in the artistic world, there has been little increase in visibility: the first lesbian MP in the UK 'came out' only last year. And for all the gains made, Souhami warns, 'It could always slip back; prejudice stills lurks.' ❏

Sarah A Smith is associate editor of Transitions
Diana Souhami The Trials of Radclyffe Hall *(Weidenfeld & Nicolson, July 1998, £20)*

Bordering on peace

Edited by *Michael Foley* & *John O'Farrell*

It is cold comfort for the families of those
who died in Omagh, and for the community
of that small town itself, but the response to
the horror of Saturday 15 August does show
the strength of a process that is backed by the
unequivocal will of the people. Not even a
tragedy as horrific as the Omagh massacre has
derailed the peace process.

True, it has put a number of the leading figures under pressure, but the will of the people as expressed in two plebiscites, north and south, on 22 May has remained in place.

The horror of Omagh has forced the people of Ireland to look at the nature of democracy when under attack by a fascist group gang whose aim is to undermine that democracy. The 'Real IRA' members who carried out the bombing are not mindless murderers. They see themselves as representing the authentic republican tradition that goes back to 1916. Their mandate comes from the Easter Rising, the election of Sinn Fein in 1918, and the programme of the first *Dail* (Parliament) of 1919. Whether one agrees with them or not, it is their political ideology that makes them so dangerous.

There has always been a strong anti-democratic strain within Irish republicanism: self determination, it holds, is inalienable and no one has the right to compromise on that. For these people the fact of the massive turnout on 22 May makes not a whit of difference. For others, including most republicans, the mandate has changed since the people of the whole island voted on the same day for the first time since 1918.

The debate about democracy has been most painful for those living in the Republic. Its citizens have been proud of their democracy and have been able to compare it favourably with the north for the past 70 years. Since the peace process and, in particular, since Omagh it has had to debate what sort of political response to both the peace process and continued violence is the most appropriate.

That response has included the introduction of the toughest anti-terrorist legislation since the foundation of the state. While concern about the civil liberties implications has been raised by both the Irish Council for Civil Liberties and the Northern Ireland Women's Forum most people have accepted that extraordinary events demand extraordinary measures and that draconian legislation, possibly even internment without trial, is a price they must pay to defend democracy. For purely pragmatic reasons, internment was not included in the new measures: it is thought unlikely to be effective.

The process was never going to be easy. It would have been a naive soul indeed who believed that 30 years of violence would simply end because of the Good Friday Agreement. What no one thought, though, was that it would take the death of the little Quinn brothers to show up the splits and contradictions in unionism and the Orange Order, and the death of 28 men, woman and children in Omagh to unite both sides in Northern Ireland and to commit the people of the Republic wholeheartedly to the process. Nor did it occur to anyone in the post-referendum optimism, that Northern Ireland would suffer its worst atrocity in the 30 years of the present troubles.

The peace process is not over: is has hardly begun. It has, however, already forced a fresh look at relationships between north and south as well as with those living on the neighbouring island. Rather than simply making Britain an object of suspicion, the process is opening up debates about nationalism, history, being European, and allowing the exploration of new and more interesting relationships with Scotland, Wales and England.

Former President Mary Robinson spoke at her inauguration of a fifth province of Ireland, the 'province of the imagination' that extends into and beyond the four historic provinces of Connaught, Munster, Leinster and Ulster.

The writer and journalist Fintan O'Toole has argued that the language of the Good Friday Agreement owes more to the traditional language of poetry rather than the two-faced pieties of diplomatic-speak. It could even be argued that the next significant step for the island after the turmoil of the past few months is for a 'fourth strand' to be inaugurated: a strand reaching beyond the geography of the territorial dispute and into a collective pooling of imaginative resources of the people of these two islands. Maybe those who hold themselves to be Irish and those who are British should now aspire towards a new form of unification, a unification of the intellect and imagination.

The bombing of Omagh forced the pace of change. While we were preparing for a winter of political shenanigans from the Northern Ireland Assembly, and for discussions on precisely what North-South institutions would be established and what institutions would have to be demolished under the Agreement, Omagh forced us to confront our willingness to defend and define the post Good Friday Agreement democracy and to acknowledge the lengths the people of the island of Ireland were willing to go to defend it. ❏

Michael Foley is media correspondent of the Irish Times *and a regular contributor to* Index. *John O'Farrell is the editor of the Belfast-based magazine* Fortnight

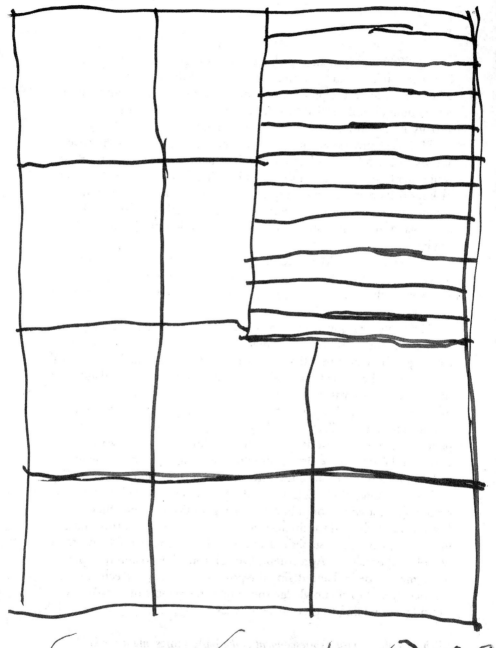

Sean Scully 8.18.9

The Glamoured

Brightening brightness, alone on the road, she appears,
Crystalline crystal and sparkle of blue in green eyes,
Sweetness of sweetness in her unembittered young voice
And a high colour dawning behind the pearl of her face.

Ringlets and ringlets, a curl in every tress
Of her fair hair trailing and brushing the dew on the grass;
And a gem from her birthplace far in the high universe
Outglittering glass and gracing the groove of her breasts.

News that was secret she whispered to soothe her aloneness,
News of one due to return and reclaim his true place,
News of the ruin of those who had cast him in darkness,
News that was awesome, too awesome to utter in verse.

My head got lighter and lighter but still I approached her,
Enthralled by her thraldom, helplessly held and bewildered,
Choking and calling Christ's name: then she fled in a shimmer
To Luachra Fort where only the glamoured can enter.

I hurtled and hurled myself madly following after
Over keshes and marshes and mosses and treacherous moors
And arrived at that stronghold unsure about how I had got there,
That earthwork of earth the orders of magic once reared.

A gang of thick louts were shouting loud insults and jeering
And a curly-haired coven in fits of sniggers and sneers:
Next thing I was taken and cruelly shackled in fetters
As the breasts of the maiden were groped by a thick-witted boor.

I tried then as hard as I could to make her hear truth,
How wrong she was to be linked to that lazarous swine
When the pride of the pure Scottish stock, a prince of the blood,
Was ardent and eager to wed her and make her his bride.

When she heard me, she started to weep, but pride was the cause
Of those tears that came wetting her cheeks and shone in her eyes;
Then she sent me a guard to guide me out of the fortress,
Who'd appeared to me, lone on the road, a brightening brightness.

Calamity, shock, collapse, heartbreak and grief
To think of her sweetnes, her beauty, her mildness, her life
Defiled at the hands of a hornmaster sprung from riff-raff,
And no hope of redress till the lions ride back on the wave.

Aodhgan O'Rathaille, translated by Seamus Heaney

SEAMUS HEANEY

'The Glamoured' is my translation of *Gile na Gile* (literally Brightness of Brightness), one of the most famous Irish poems of the early eighteenth century. It is a classic example of a genre know as the *aisling* (pronounced ashling) which was as characteristic of Irish-language poetry in the late seventeenth and eighteenth centuries as rhymed satire was in England at the same time.

The *aisling* was in effect a mixture of *samizdat* and allegory, a form which mixed political message with passionate vision. After the devastations and repressions brought about by the armies of Oliver Cromwell and KingWilliam, the native Irish population became subject to the Penal Laws, a system of legislation as deliberately conceived as apartheid, enacted against them specifically as catholics by the Irish parliament (representing the 'Protestant interest' which took control after William of Orange's victory over the forces of the catholic Stuart king, James II, at the Battle of the Boyne). The native Irish aristocracy fled – and were ever afterwards know as The Wild Geese – and dreams of redress got transferred into poetry.

Politically, the *aisling* kept alive the hope of a Stuart restoration which would renew the fortunes of the native Irish. Symbolically, this was expressed in the ancient form of a dream encounter in which the poet meets a beautiful woman in some lonely place. This woman is at one and the same time an apparition of the spirit of Ireland and a muse figure who entrances him completely. She inevitably displays signs of grief and tells a story of how she is in thrall to some heretical foreign brute, but the poem usually ends with a promise – which history will not fulfil – of liberation in the form of a Stuart prince coming to her relief from beyond the seas.

Aodhgan O'Rathaille (c1675-1729) is one of the last great voices of the native Irish tradition, Dantesque in his anger and hauteur, a voice crying in the more or less literal wilderness of the Gaelic outback, at once the master of outrage and the witness of desolation. ❏

Seamus Heaney is a Derry-born poet and winner of the Nobel Prize for Literature.

JOHN O'FARRELL

Murdering the future

The bombs in Ballymoney and Omagh were designed to wreck forever the hope of peace in Ireland. The Good Friday Agreement was the target of a minority on both sides who voted 'No' to peace and 'Yes' to the destructive violence into which they are locked. The bombs backfired: by targeting children, the paramilitary on both sides not only murdered the future in a literal sense, they sealed their own fates as those who had marked 'Yes' on a ballot paper found the courage in grief to stand up and make their voices heard

Fire has an elemental hold on cultures around the world. Northern Ireland is no exception. The eleventh of July on the local calender is bonfire night, when Ulster protestants commence the highlight of the public celebrations of their reformed faith, loyalty to the British monarch and belief in the union with Great Britain.

For weeks beforehand, kids in loyalist areas collect wood, old furniture, anything that will burn. The detritus of flammable leftovers is painstakenly built into enormous structures, comparable only to the massive bonfires held at Las Fallas in Valencia every May, topped with an effigy of the Pope, or some current hate figure (such as Gerry Adams), and flowing with petrol-soaked Irish tricolours.

At midnight, the flames start, egged on by hundreds on the wastegrounds of Belfast, the edges of villages, or the open spaces of suburban housing estates. Loyalist bands compete with huge sound systems for the greater decibel count, as the beer and cider flow in the biggest street parties in the province.

After a few hours' sleep, or none at all, the revellers change into their best suits, don their orange sashes, and prepare to march all day in the Twelfth celebrations that commemorate the victory of the protestant King William over a catholic army at the Battle of the Boyne in 1690. The loyalist bandsmen dress up in their colourful uniforms and accompany the marchers, competing with other bands for arrangements, originality of repertoire and choreography. The spectacle brings thousands out onto the streets and in hamlets. The noise and colour make an awesome spectacle.

This year's affirmation of faith and fatherland had a cloud hanging over it. The smoke from the firebomb that roasted three children alive subdued the Twelfth and changed forever the role of the Orange Order in the running of what was once 'The Orange State'.

The slow-motion coup d'état at Drumcree, where Orangemen came perilously close to wrecking Northern Ireland's peace agreement, ended in the ashes of Carnany Park. The cost was more than three young lives. The threat of the 'Orange card', the Order's ability to mobilise thousands and scupper any change to protestant hegemony, has been bluffed by Tony Blair. For over 150 years, the Orange Order has been the bedrock of unionist ideology. Now, as the various pillars of unionism have split, the foundation itself is giving way. How and why has this happened? What, if anything can replace it? Is Northern Ireland rid finally of the forces that used sectarianism as the stick to beat democracy and equality? Or does the agreement signed on Good Friday contain the seeds of the next round of conflict?

The last thing anyone heard 10-year-old Richard Quinn say was this: 'Mammy, me feet are burning, me feet are burning'. Richard, like his brothers Lee, Mark and Jason, was rarely brought to church. Their mother is catholic, but neither Chrissie nor her ex-husband, John Dillon, bothered much with religion. They were a poor family, like most of their neighbours on the Carnany estate, a social dumping-ground on the outskirts of Ballymoney in north Antrim. The estate has about 70 per cent unemployment and 85 per cent of its families are protestant. Like most estates that boast such figures, the kerbstones are painted red, white and blue, and gable-end graffiti notify strangers of the presence of the Ulster Volunteer Force and the Ulster Freedom Fighters. Bunting the colour of the kerbstones hangs across the streets, and most houses fly the flags of the United Kingdom, Ulster or the Orange Order.

A Union Jack flew from the house next door to the Quinn's. They had been up late, celebrating the eleventh night, having returned home from the bonfire the Quinn children had helped collect wood for with the other kids on the estate. At 4:30am they heard an explosion and ran out to warn the Quinns. They got Chrissie and her protestant boyfriend out, but no-one could reach the back bedroom where the three boys were. Chrissie's boyfriend climbed onto the back kitchen roof to try to reach the boys. He smashed his fist through the blackened window, but it was too late. Overcome by heat and fumes, he collapsed and fell off the roof.

He was still in hospital when the funeral cortege left the catholic church at Ballymoney. Thirteen-year-old Lee, in his best blue tracksuit, looked dazed as he held his grandmother's hand. The boys were buried near her home in Rasharkin, 15 miles from the fire. Chrissie Quinn never wants to see Ballymoney ever again.

The Member of Parliament for North Antrim is the Reverend Dr Ian KR Paisley. He does not attend catholic services, believing that even funeral services are acts of apostasy. Instead, Dr Paisley went to Drumcree, where Portadown Orangemen were in the ninth day of their stand-off with the security forces who were blocking their 'traditional route' from Drumcree church to Portadown Orange Hall down the catholic Garvaghy Road. Dr Paisley told the 2,000 Orangemen and their supporters that the triple murder of the Quinn boys was nothing to do with the 'peaceful and dignified protest' of the Orange Order. Their 'civil and religious liberties' had to be upheld. Blame for the violence over the previous week was the fault of the catholic residents of the Garvaghy Road, of the Independent Parades Commission who rerouted the march, of the 'pan-nationalist front' of the Irish government, of the SDLP, the Catholic Church and the IRA who 'want to destroy everything which is protestant and British in Ulster', of Mo Mowlam and Tony Blair and the British government and Bill Clinton who are working for 'a united Ireland by the back door'.

Paisley and his son, Ian Junior, briefed journalists that the Ballymoney arson attack was the work of a relative of the Quinn family. Denis Watson, County Armagh Grand Master, told Orangemen on the Twelfth that a relative had been arrested. David Jones, spokesman of the Portadown Orangemen spoke of a dark 'collusion' between loyalist paramilitaries and the security forces. All argued that the media were unfair to focus on the Quinn murders as being the responsibility of Orangeism or the protest at Drumcree. Just to be clear, the tally of the first week included 144 petrol bomb attacks on the homes of catholics or police officers, 24 shooting incidents and 45 'blast bombs' thrown at the RUC which left 76 injured. The night after Ballymoney, nine houses were petrol-bombed. All of this violence was 'condemned' by the Orange Order, who blamed 'malcontents'. When the RUC eventually moved into the fields around Drumcree church, they found dozens of blast bombs, explosive darts and a sub-machine gun. David Jones blamed 'republicans' for planting the weapons under the noses of thousands of Orangemen.

This denial of the obvious has a long lineage in unionist politics. Throughout the Troubles, loyalist paramilitaries have seen themselves as the 'cutting edge' of unionism in its struggle against nationalism. In return, they have been ostracised, condemned and scorned by the mainstream unionists of David Trimble's Ulster Unionist Party and Dr Paisley's Democratic Unionists. Nevertheless, when muscle was required, such as for the overthrow of the 1973 Sunningdale Agreement, the call was answered. Likewise in the aftermath of the 1985 Anglo-Irish Agreement, loyalist paramilitaries provided the numbers for the roadblocks and demonstrations, and the guns for random, terrifying attacks on the catholic population.

The UVF and UFF ceasefires of October 1994 ended this cosy, hands-off (some allege back-room) relationship. The emergence of political parties representing the two main loyalist paramilitaries gave a political voice to men who had previously been spoken for, and occasionally at, by their 'democratic' betters. The boys who never made it to Queen's University or Bible college got educated in the Maze prison, courtesy of the Open University. They spoke of a 'progressive way forward', and spoke with Sinn Fein for prisoner releases and against decommissioning. The inevitable split occurred when Billy Wright formed the Loyalist Volunteer Force. But Billy is dead, and the LVF have acquired a taste for a BMW-and-gold-chain lifestyle, paid for by 'taxing' drug dealers.

The other pillars of unionism, the political parties and the protestant churches are hopelessly split over working or wrecking the Agreement. David Trimble is First Minister, about to share power with a nationalist Deputy First Minister, but has alienated half of the UUP. The Orange

Credit: Christian Schwetz

Order seemed united against the threats of the Parades Commission and the 'chilling' Agreement, and united behind the Drumcree protests. Tens of thousands massed each night, and many wondered if the fortifications could hold a determined push. Orangemen spoke gleefully of up to 100,000 turning up on the Twelfth. Ballymoney stopped that. At most 3,000 turned up, the rest ashamed and disheartened. Everyone, except the Portadown 'brethren' knew the game was up, and that they should heed the advice of David Trimble and 'go home'.

A remarkable thing has happened. The murder of the Quinn boys seems to have struck a chord unheard before among 'middle protestantism'. The ability of mainstream, middle-class unionists to psychologically distance themselves from the killing of, say, three catholic taxi drivers by 'loyalist thugs', has backfired; a collective sense of guilt clouds a political culture based on the right to say 'no' endlessly.

Northern catholics recognise this guilt. They have felt it over La Mon, Enniskillen, Warrington and the lynching of two corporals on camera in 1988. It could be due to what some call 'catholic group thinking'. If that is so, Ballymoney has punctured the individualist protestant ethos that made loyalist atrocities explicable as the work of aberrant individuals, incapable or unworthy of speaking for protestants as a group.

All that is left now is the Agreement. It has been endorsed twice, by referendum and the Assembly election in which over 70 per cent voted for pro-Agreement candidates. The new majority is not protestant unionists, but catholics and protestants supporting the sharing of power between unionism and nationalism. The minority are that half of unionism that fantasises about a return to the old Stormont, 'a protestant parliament for a protestant people'. Drumcree was an attempt to scupper the new deal by driving a sectarian wedge between pro-Agreement catholics and protestants. It almost succeeded, until Ballymoney forced the 50 per cent of unionists in favour to find their voices, and tell the 'no' men to 'go home'.

Drumcree really was the last stand. It was an attempt to 'strangle the Agreement at birth', as one Orange leader put it. It was an attempt to turn the clock back: literally to murder the future. And the future it killed was its own. Orangeism is ruptured, a burned-out case, trapped on the funeral pyre it built for itself, fuelled by the blood of Ballymoney.

Ghosts

At 3.10pm, on 15 August 1998, Omagh stopped being a small market town in County Tyrone. It became a cypher, a symbol for pain, loss, dashed hopes and dignity under incredible duress. Just when it seemed that hope had prevailed with the Agreement, came the bomb.

More people were killed in Omagh than by any other bomb in 30 years. More catholics were killed by the Real IRA than by loyalists in the whole of 1998. Unlike the surgical bigotry in which young men were the main victims of random and planned shootings, the bulk of the 28 dead were mothers and children, teenage boys and girls, grandmothers and grandfathers, the demographic mix one expects to see out shopping on a Saturday afternoon.

The fathers arrived at the local hospital. They stood, dazed, unknowing of the fate of their loved ones, with other fathers, friends and family. They quietly asked nurses, priests, chaplains, bloodsoaked witnesses to the carnage who had brought the dead and injured in their cars, buses, vans, if they knew anything. If they were alive, maimed or lost. If they were in that hospital, or any of the hospitals in Northern Ireland or across the border in Donegal which had opened its emergency units for the hundreds of injured.

They went to Omagh Leisure Centre, which acted as the information centre, where names were pasted up on boards, giving the location of the hospital ward. Some were approached by a policeman and priest, and knew they were about to hear the unsayable. Then they went home, and made the arrangements for the funeral.

After the roar, the silence. In the town centre, people walked slowly towards the bridge at Campsie Street and stared past the blue-and-white tape and the army Land Rovers, into the mess of Market Street. Despite the demolition of Roy Kells' shop, outside which the Vauxhall and its 500lb cargo exploded, the damage seemed small compared to other bombs that had demolished whole streets, such as the one left in Banbridge two Saturdays before. That one injured 17 people. This one concentrated its destructive energies on the people surrounding the car. Nine people were ripped asunder buying school uniforms in Kells' shop.

The chassis of the car was all that was left, weirdly resembling the bent and buckled pushchairs scattered around the scene.

Then a quiet sob would emerge, and arms would appear to comfort the shaking shoulders. That Saturday evening in the Campsie Bar, the new strangers in town were asked: 'Who are you?' They didn't want to talk to reporters, who couldn't, anyway, think of any questions to ask. But the tales would pour out regardless.

That man, the one crying at the bar, he emptied his van of its contents and got as many injured as possible into it. The hospital was inundated, so he drove them to casualty in Enniskillen, 40 miles away. His van, like his hands were covered in blood, but he kept going. And now, in the comfort of his local pub, he could have the luxury of weeping. He could do no more.

That woman, who tried to give the kiss of life to a still, teenage boy; who turned him over to find no lips, nose or eyes to kiss.

The man who cradled a dying baby in his arms.

The old man who went up to the leisure centre to look for lonely victims, who might have nobody to grieve for them.

For days afterwards, I walked through the town, hearing stories, followed by sobs. The people of Omagh did not resent the huge media pack. There were no charges that we were colonising their grief, or exploiting their pain. Those who spoke did so to explain rather than convert. There were no big lessons, just incomprehension that any person or group would or could do such a thing.

Some days after, I spoke with a man who had lost no-one. He used to drink too much. He had not been in a pub for years. That night he was. He hadn't slept since Saturday. He was up in the Leisure Centre, holding hands, trying to comfort. He was also waiting for news of two business friends who he was convinced were dead. On the Sunday night, he saw one enter the Centre with his wife. He called him and, rushing to embrace him, he saw his other friend, who he thought was also missing. He stopped, and stepped back. 'Ghosts,' he cried. 'You're both ghosts. You're not here.' But they were.

Then he left me, to see some other friends who had lost a son and would bury him the following morning. ❏

JO'F

LUKE GIBBONS

Radical memory

By refusing to see the past as over and done with, especially the past of the victims of history, commemoration becomes radical memory, not a consolation for things past nor an exercise in futile nostalgia

When Chairman Mao was asked on one occasion what he thought of the French Revolution, he answered cryptically: 'It's too early to say'. The same might be said of contemporary Irish responses to the bicentenary of the 1798 rebellion, the greatest political insurrection in Irish history.

It is strange how the dim vistas of a distant future were already present in the minds of those shaping the revolutionary legacy of the 1790s. Preparing for a French invasion of Ireland, Wolfe Tone, the leader of the United Irishmen who organised the rebellion, wrote that if they did not get it right this time, it would set Ireland back for the next 200 years. Taking him at his word, a state official wrote to a military leader engaged in the savage reprisals following the rebellion that they would teach the rebels a lesson that would serve them for the whole of the century that would end with the year 2000.

It was as if a time mechanism, or delay switch, was built into the horrors of the 1790s from the outset, ensuring that the unfolding drama of events would not take its course for centuries to come. This has far-reaching consequences for the way memory in Ireland operates on the minds of the living. The bicentenary of 1798 – as indeed the centenary commemorations of 1898 – is not an aspect of the heritage industry, or the mummified past of museums, but a part of what has come to be termed 'the unfinished business' of history itself. It may be that only now has Irish society belatedly caught up with the breadth of vision of the radical project envisaged by the United Irishmen 200 years ago.

The United Irishmen, founded by Wolfe Tone and others in Belfast
and Dublin in 1791, were inspired by the Enlightenment principles of
liberty, equality and fraternity that informed the American and French
revolutions. But they also brought a new complexity to their conception
of liberty that addresses some of the most intractable ethnic and cultural
conflicts in the world today. Unlike their counterparts in America and
France, the Irish revolutionaries embraced the concept of cultural as well
as individual human rights, particularly as these affected the rights of
dispossessed, indigenous peoples.

The Enlightenment, in its dominant metropolitan modes, not only
excluded 'primitive' societies or 'peoples without history' from its remit,
but under the principles of progress and universality, actively promoted
their destruction. It was for this reason that the benefits of the new
American republic were not extended to African-American slaves, and
that the only mention of Native Americans in the Declaration of
Independence is as 'merciless savages'. By contrast, the United Irishmen
sought to include the 'wretched of the earth' in Ireland – the despised
culture of the mass of the Gaelic-speaking catholic peasantry – within
their vision of liberty, thus laying the basis for the revival of native
culture. This sympathy with the 'excluded other' was not confined to
Ireland but also extended to slavery – an issue on which they publicly
disagreed with Thomas Jefferson – even embraced the plight of the
Native American Indian.

This was not just an exercise in romantic nostalgia, if by that is meant
the idealisation of exotic cultures precisely because they could no longer
participate in the political and economic affairs of the real world. This
was the fate of 'the noble savage' in romantic primitivism and of the
Gaelic Highlands in Scottish romanticism in the aftermath of the
crushing defeat of Culloden. But notwithstanding the scale of the
catastrophe in Ireland – over 30,000 were killed in one month, more
than in the first few years of the French Revolution – 1798 was no
Culloden where Irish culture was concerned. While there was no
glossing over the trauma of defeat, there was also no relapse into fatalism,
or an enervating Celtic melancholia.

Commemoration became radical memory, not a consolation for
things past.

Thus, in the legacy bequeathed by 1798, even the backward look of
romanticism was imbued with Enlightenment principles of optimism

and modernity. The United Irishmen's programme, through their alliance with the mass agrarian movement of the oppressed catholic peasantry known as the Defenders, represented the first fully fledged attempt to bring subaltern classes, and the cultural diversity they represented, into the realm of rights and equality. Like Anteus in the ancient Greek myth, the strength of the movement grew from its contact with the soil.

Ironically, it is this aspect of the United Irishmen that has drawn most criticism from revisionist historians and commentators today. Their ideas were fine in principle, it is argued, but they were too utopian and got bogged down in the quagmire of sectarian politics in Ireland. What is notable, however, about the United Irishmen is that their ideals were never abstractions but, in contrast to the universalism of their American and French counterparts, were rooted in cultural diversity and were, accordingly, adapted to the local contingencies of time and place. This was an Enlightenment that sought to give cultures back their own voices, rather than speaking on their behalf from some more 'advanced' social or cultural vantage point.

This visionary project came unstuck not because of local sectarian animosities, but because it threatened the might of the British empire in the midst of the first modern, global war with revolutionary France. Though the rebellion was defeated, it was not discredited. By refusing to see the past as over and done with, especially the past of the victims of history, the United Irishmen had cultivated a form of radical memory in which even their own defeat would not be the end of the affair. Not least of the ironies of history is that on 23 May 1998, exactly 200 years after the outbreak of the rebellion, the results of the Referendum on the Peace Process were announced, with considerable majorities on both side of the border in favour of a new political way forward in Ireland. ❏

Luke Gibbons is a writer and academic. He teaches at Dublin City University

ROBERT FISK

Borders

There is nothing unique about Ireland's border problems; yesterday's border conflicts are today's hotspots from the Lebanon to Yugoslavia

'The Border' is part of the lexicon of Irish politics, even for those who have never crossed it. The Border – it's as if we have ceased to think of it as an international line on a map, even though it is an international frontier. And although it follows a few appropriate burrens and drumlin tops and an occasional river – the Foyle is the largest – the Irish Border is a strange old line, like the Bosnian-Croatian frontier and the boundaries of most Middle East nations.

For the Irish are not unique in the oddness of their border. The French as well as the British spent two happy years playing around with frontiers in the Middle East between 1918 and 1920. They chopped up the old *vilayet* of Syria, created a mandate territory called Palestine, another called Transjordan – on the other side of the river Jordan, so here at least was a sensible frontier, marked by a waterway – and yet a third called Iraq. There was a little problem – and had been for more than two decades already – over the indecisive nature of Iraq's southern border, the frontier with Kuwait, which had once been an Ottoman province of Iraq.

The British controlled all these frontiers, as they controlled the new nations within them, under the 'sacred trust', as it was then called, of the League of Nations, the predecessor of our old friend the United Nations. North of Palestine, the French took over and out of what was left of Syria decided to create an entirely new nation. In the mountains above the southern Syrian coastline, there had, for many centuries, lived a Christian community of Maronite Catholics, a community that, after a civil war with the Druze in 1860, had come to rely on France for

*Border landscape, Leitrim-Fermanagh –
Credit: Frankie Quinn*

protection. They spoke French, gave themselves French names, sent their children to be educated at French universities, 'francophiled' themselves so thoroughly that even to this day many of them speak better French than Arabic. In Northern Ireland, too, there existed a population that felt – or thought it felt – more British than Irish and that relied on Britain for 'protection' against its neighbours to the south, a people who were educated at Protestant-dominated universities or English colleges.

France saw the Lebanese Maronites as 'their' people – just as British Tories saw the Protestants as 'their' Irish – and the Maronites of the western part of Syria spoke of France as their 'mother country'. And

when France decided to divide up its mandate territory, as the British were doing farther south, they decided that the Christian Maronites of Syria should have a state of their own, named after the Lebanon. A one-armed veteran of the World War I, General Henri Gouraud, helped to draw the frontiers of this new country. 'Greater Lebanon' it would be called. The Patriarch of the Maronite Church fought hard at the 1919 Versailles peace conference for the biggest country he could get for his Christians.

For the Maronites would be a privileged community in Lebanon; they would run the country and, after independence, would supply all its

presidents, under a French-inspired covenant that gave political power to the Christians in perpetuity. The Christians would run the banks and the port as well as the most powerful ministries. And their country would include much more than Mount Lebanon. The French took from Syria the cities of Beirut, Sidon, Tyre and Tripoli and gave them to the new Christian-run state of Lebanon. As for the Muslims of this new 'Lebanon', they had given their views on all this, along with the Christians, to an American League of Nations delegation, two US scholars who dutifully toured the villages and towns of this new state before the French drew their lines on the map. The vast majority of the population opposed a partition from Syria. But General Gouraud went ahead and created Lebanon.

At almost the same time, another World War I veteran, Captain James Craig, was trying to create another new statelet well over 2,000 miles away, with yet another 'mother country' to which this statelet would pronounce its loyalty. Several Maronites had asked for Lebanon to be not just a

One of the estimated 270 cross border roads that have been blocked by the British since 1971 – Credit: Frankie Quinn

French mandate territory but an integral part of France itself, part of 'France d'outre mer' like Algeria. The French wisely turned them down. Craig had only to demand to remain British in 1920 for it to be so; the territory that was to become known as 'Northern Ireland' had already been part of 'the United Kingdon of Great Britain and Ireland'. And there was another intriguing difference between General Gouraud and Captain Craig.

The French allowed the Maronites to take from Syria as many square miles as they could control, provided they were able to maintain a Christian majority in that territory. And the Maronites, pleased to have their own country, paid no heed to the numerical weakness of this majority. By 1932, this was wafer thin; which is why there has been no census since, for such a poll would demonstrate that Lebanon has long had a Muslim majority and this might change those carefully drawn frontiers.

Captain Craig tried the reverse of the Gouraud policy. He chose to hold on to only those areas that could maintain a protestant majority in the years to come. Northern Ireland would always remain protestant because protestants would always outnumber catholics behind the border – a temporary border so the Irish on both sides of it were told at the time – which would exclude those areas of the old historical Ulster whose protestant populations were outnumbered (or in danger of being outnumbered) by catholics. So 70,000 protestants in Cavan, Monaghan and Donegal were abandoned by the new province of 'Ulster'.

'The figures will at once show where the difficulties come in,' Sir Edward Carson told the British House of Commons in 1920. 'We have to refer in these matters to protestant and catholic because these are really the burning questions ... while you would leave out 70,000 who are in these three counties, you would bring from those counties into the northern province an additional 250,000 Roman Catholics.' So while Captain Craig was giving up any claim to Monaghan, Cavan and Donegal, General Gouraud was

Confrontation between British soldiers and protesters on the Armagh/Louth border, March 1996 – Credit: Frankie Quinn

claiming Beirut, Sidon, Tripoli and the entire Bekaa Valley as part of his newly created state in the Middle East. Captain Craig limited his state to maintain a sectarian ascendancy, and turned his minority into second-class citizens. In Lebanon, General Gouraud enlarged the nation he was creating to extend sectarian power, and produced a state in which the eventual majority were second-class citizens. Both creations were to end in tears.

Nation-building, as we would come to call it 70 years later, was about frontiers in those years after the World War I. And Winston Churchill's wearying expression – that the dreary steeples of Fermanagh and Tyrone re-emerged after the flood of the 1914-18 war with the integrity of their quarrel intact – applied in both the Middle East and in what was about to become Yugoslavia. We sorted our way through the tribal alliances of the old Ottoman Middle East – to our own advantage of course – and allowed the new nations of central and southern Europe to draw their own frontiers in the wreckage of the same Ottoman empire in the Balkans.

For just when Northern Ireland and Lebanon were coming into existence, the world also gave birth to a country called Yugoslavia, a kingdom fought over by domestic communists and fascists, which broke apart the moment Germany invaded Yugoslavia in 1941. The Nazis let loose the Croats against the Serbs and encouraged the Muslims to join the Croats against the Serbs, enlisting many other Bosnian Muslims to fight on Germany's side against the Soviet Union. In the same year, 1941, Lebanon was invaded by the allies and French troops loyal to Vichy fought the Free French inside the country. Had Ireland been invaded in the World War II, there would surely have been a civil conflict in the island as Irishmen took opposing sides.

So it is around these borders in the Middle East, in Yugoslavia and in Ireland – all laid down in the aftermath of the 1914-1918 war – that conflict has continued ever since; in the Middle East, in what was and is no longer Yugoslavia and in Ireland. Other frontiers were drawn at that

Local residents groups (Border Busters) dismantling one of the barricades that blocked many cross border roads, Sept 1994 – Credit: Frankie Quinn

time in Transcaucasia – one of them divided an Armenian mountain chain from Christian Armenia and gave it to Muslim Azerbaijan. This mountainous area is called Nagorny Karabakh and remains a focus for political unrest to this day.

None of these borders were drawn for the old European purpose – as defensive frontiers against aggression. True, the River Tigris partly divides Syria from Iraq, the River Jordan divides Jordan from the West Bank and a few miles of the River Foyle divides Northern Ireland from the Irish Republic. But the borders are largely indefensible. Which is why Iraq found it so easy to invade Kuwait in 1990, why Israel found it so simple to conquer the Arab territory of the West Bank in 1967, why Syria's forces could sweep into Lebanon in 1976. The Serbs drove without hindrance across the Croatian plain east of Vukovar in 1991, although they could not cross the only natural frontier, the River Sava that divides Serbian Bosnia from Croatia. In Ireland, 'the Border' provided no protection for those who lived on either side.

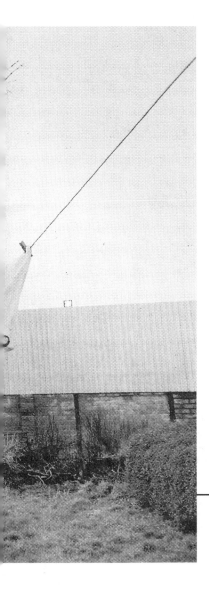

Thus the European powers of the immediate post-World War I era fuelled the conflicts that have continued to preoccupy us to this day. Europeans created the Arab nations of the Middle East in order, supposedly, to satisfy their demand for independence after 1918 – but we gave them frontiers that would render them permanently vulnerable. They would need our help if they were threatened. In the Balkans, the creation of Yugoslavia was a useful buffer between the powers of central Europe and the Islamic world, which

British Army base at Crossmaglen, Co Armagh, June 1995 – Credit: Frankie Quinn

began beyond the south-eastern frontier of Greece. In Ireland, where demands for independence from British rule had attracted the US President who supported the demands of freedom for the Arabs, Woodrow Wilson, a new border was created.

Nor was this border merely a concession to the protestants of Northern Ireland. Throughout the 1930s, Winston Churchill was to

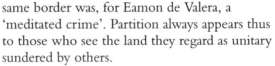

remind Britons of their strategic interest in the north-eastern corner of Ireland, a base for the Royal Navy's Atlantic operations in time of war if the Irish Free State refused to participate in a war against Germany.

In 1939, with the Treaty ports of Cobh, Beerhaven and Lough Swilly handed to the then Free State, Northern Ireland did briefly – for the last time – acquire strategic importance for Britain. The creation of that same border was, for Eamon de Valera, a 'meditated crime'. Partition always appears thus to those who see the land they regard as unitary sundered by others.

John Hume, leader of northern Ireland's Social and Democratic Liberal Party, might have spoken for them all when he told the UK *Independent* on 27 October 1993 that 'Britain came to Ireland in the seventeenth century because of Irish links with Spain. The Act of Union in 1800 was Britain's response to the links with France, fearing that Ireland could now be used as a back door by her European enemies. That's all gone now ... The nature of the problem has changed, but the legacy remains and the legacy is a divided people.'

And it's people who have rights, not territory. ❏

Robert Fisk *is the Beirut-based Middle East correspondent of the London* Independent

Frankie Quinn *is a freelance photographer based in Belfast. These photographs are from a study of the border region made over several years*

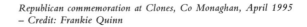

Republican commemoration at Clones, Co Monaghan, April 1995 – Credit: Frankie Quinn

DOMINIC BRYAN & NEIL JARMAN

Parades and power

Whenever political change in the north threatens their centuries-old hegemony, the protestant marching season takes on a special significance. This year's Orange parades marched to confrontation to the fading tune of a dying order

In July 1995, within a year of the ceasefires, the world's media once again turned their attention to Northern Ireland. This was not a straightforward story of bombs and shootings, but a more complex – and to many incomprehensible – affair involving a dispute over the right of the protestant Orange Order to parade past the catholic estates on the Garvaghy Road in the largely protestant town of Portadown.

The Orangemen were returning along their 'traditional' route from a service in Drumcree Church to mark the Battle of the Boyne of 1690 when England's protestant King William of Orange defeated the army of the catholic King James of Scotland. The Royal Ulster Constabulary (RUC) decided to re-route the parade because of protests by local residents but the Orangemen insisted they would remain at the church until they were allowed down the road.

After two days, a tentative agreement allowed the parade to proceed but catholics were angered when two leading Unionist politicians - Ian Paisley and David Trimble - proclaimed their arrival in the town as a victory for the Orangemen.

The second 'Siege of Drumcree', in 1996, led to five days of rioting and civil disturbance as Orangemen blocked roads across Northern Ireland. When the chief constable decided to force the parade along the road, the police used violence and plastic bullets to clear the residents; nationalists across the north rioted in protest. In 1997, the RUC again used violence to clear residents from the road and allow Orangemen their right to parade.

Many people outside Northern Ireland find these events difficult to comprehend. Yet the parades have played an important role in the development of ethnic identities in Northern Ireland and such public events have been a key arena in which relations of power are articulated. In a society that is increasingly segregated, many Orange parades are seen by catholic residents as an annual invasion. In contrast exercising the right to march their 'traditional' routes symbolises for Orangemen that Northern Ireland remains firmly within the UK. Members of the Orange Order argue that it exists to 'defend and promote the protestant faith', but for many catholics it promotes little more than sectarianism.

The Orange Order was founded near Portadown in 1795 following recurrent clashes between protestant and catholic groups and soon drew support from all sections of the Protestant community. In the second half of the nineteenth century the Order was at the centre of opposition to

Home Rule and organised 'monster' parades on the Twelfth of July, the anniversary of the Boyne. After partition in 1920, it became a powerful unifying force for protestants in the new Northern Ireland. Membership of the Orange Order was virtually a requirement for any Unionist politician seeking to advance his career; for catholics the Order symbolised the oppression they felt in the new state. Orange parades, functioning virtually as rituals of state, represented the domination of the protestant population in the public sphere.

In the 1960s, the campaign for equal rights for catholics challenged this control of public space. Civil rights demonstrations provoked violent reactions when they tried to invoke the same rights to march as were claimed by protestants; tension at parades became common. The Troubles began when rioting broke out following a parade in Derry in August 1969 held by the Apprentice Boys – a protestant organisation similar in nature to the Orange Order. British soldiers were brought onto the streets to try to contain the violence and soon the demand for equal rights had been eclipsed by a military campaign against the state.

Through the 1970s and 1980s, Orange parades became an ever more assertive expression of militant loyalism as an increasing number of 'blood and thunder' flute bands appeared at these events. Many of the bands displayed flags, instruments and uniforms carrying symbols of allegiance to loyalist paramilitary groups the Ulster Volunteer Force and the Ulster Defence Association. Although parades are perceived as 'traditional' and unchanging events, they have always been made to reflect contemporary politics.

Parades have persistently been the focus of disputes in the north of Ireland but at times of political transition they have become particularly significant. Their role as a site for public political confrontation intensified after the paramilitary ceasefires were called in 1994. Residents' groups appeared in a number of areas to oppose Orange parades. As the ceasefires made it easier for new political alliances to be forged, the groups drew support from a cross-section of the Nationalist community. At the same time, the RUC – albeit a 95 per cent protestant force containing significant numbers of Orangemen – became less willing to continue their historical role of protecting Orange parades. Although the Drumcree parade was allowed to follow its

Derry Apprentice Boys singing 'God save the Queen', July 1996 –
Credit: Frankie Quinn

'traditional route', many other Orange parades were blocked or re-routed between 1995 and 1997. In past years up to a dozen annual parades had passed along the lower Ormeau Road area of Belfast, but in 1997 all were forcibly or voluntarily re-routed.

The role of the Orange Order within political life in Northern Ireland is changing. Membership has declined from 100,000 to less than half that figure and the Order has become increasingly less important as an institution of political and economic patronage. Its organisational structure is a hierarchy of private lodges, district lodges, county lodges up to the Grand Lodge of Ireland, but its authority structure is weak, with power effectively residing with local lodges rather than with the Grand Lodge. This, along with the diversity of its membership, has made it slow to react in a dynamic political environment.

Nevertheless, Orangeism is still a significant force in the north. Members join for a combination of political, religious, social and cultural reasons and Orange halls remain important in the social life of many protestant communities. The large majority of the 2,500 loyalist parades that take place each year are uncontroversial and play an important role in community life. This helps to explain why an otherwise minor parade such as that at Drumcree, can have such a resonance for many within the protestant community.

Orange parades remain a crucial element in defining control of public space. Most Catholics still see them as triumphalist and sectarian displays, yet for many Protestants they provide a political, religious, historical and social focus for an otherwise fragmented and disparate community.

Since March this year, a Parades Commission has been empowered to make decisions over the right to march, and in July it re-routed the Drumcree parade. Protestants still hold 10 times more parades each year than the catholic community but the forces of the state are far less willing than in earlier years unquestioningly to protect the rights of the Orange Order. The disputes in Portadown and elsewhere give clear public expression to the changing relations of power in Northern Ireland. ❏

Dominic Bryan and *Neal Jarman*, *at the University of Ulster, are the leading academic authorities on the Orange Order in Northern Ireland. Neal Jarman's book, 'Material Conflict: Parades and Visual Displays in Northern Ireland', is published by Berg (Oxford)*

MICHAEL FOLEY

A people's press

Local papers still drive news and debate in Northern Ireland, more so than on the mainland. Every facet of the community finds a voice

It is mid-morning in Derry city. A woman enters a newsagent's shop and goes to take a copy of the *Sun*. 'Not that one, the one to your right, Mrs O'Doherty,' says the newsagent. He directs Mrs O'Doherty to the Irish edition of the *Sun*, which is lying beside the standard UK edition. Mrs O'Doherty is, of course, a catholic and the newsagent knows that in Northern Ireland the newspaper you buy identifies you and tells an awful lot about you.

The same Mrs O'Doherty would, of course, also buy the *Derry Journal*, but never the *Londonderry Sentinel*. She might buy the *Irish News*, but never the *News Letter*. She might possibly buy the *Belfast Telegraph*, along with her protestant neighbour, but probably only for the small ads.

Northern Ireland is a media-saturated society. For a population of only 1.5 million, there are two television stations, BBC Northern Ireland and UTV, local radio, three daily newspapers in Belfast, as well over 40 local newspapers. About 30 per cent of the population also receives RTE, the Republic's public-service television channels.

Throughout the peace process, the referendum campaign and the assembly elections, the media, especially the newspapers, played a significant role, both reporting and entering into debate.

Northern Ireland is an unusual place. It is strangely old-fashioned in media terms and continues to rely heavily on the print media in a way that has ceased to be the case elsewhere. People buy the newspaper that reflects their view of the world; broadcasters are forced by legislation to be balanced and impartial.

Northern Ireland's divided community also means that the market forces that drive the newspaper industry elsewhere do not always operate. Newspapers that would have closed years ago live on with dwindling circulations and survive on advertising. Advertisers, especially official sources like the many quangos, the Northern Ireland Office, the Housing Executive for instance, must all place adverts in newspapers on both sides of the community or else be accused of sectarian favouritism. It is like a subsidy put in place to ensure that all over Northern Ireland, from the big cities to the smallest town, both communities have a voice.

Some newspapers, however, went further during the difficult and protracted multi-party talks, the referendum and the elections than simply reflecting the bias and prejudice of their readers. Geoff Martin, the editor of the unionist *Belfast News Letter*, supported the Belfast Agreement, a decision that was crucial in selling the agreement to the unionist community.

'We're leading the unionist community because we don't think it's our job to sit on the fence. We've looked at the thing and decided to support it. A lot of our readers have not made that decision. Many unionists are as yet undecided,' Mr Martin said in the lead-up to the referendum.

His support for multi-party talks and the agreement shocked and surprised many unionists. It is believed his stance was possible because he was backed by the chief executive of the Mirror Group, David Montgomery, an Ulster protestant who is close to both David Trimble and the British prime minister. The Mirror bought the *News Letter* last year.

If Martin was speaking for a fragmented and confused community, as the results of the referendum showed, Tom Collins, the editor of the nationalist *Irish News,* had a more confident and united readership. 'The newspaper has two roles: one is to speak to its readership and the other to speak for it. Over the period of the peace process we have shifted from one to the other,' Collins said in an interview with *The Irish Times.*

Given that they were rival editors, he and Geoff Martin forged a unique relationship. 'Newspapers,' said Collins, 'have been closer than the politicians to the type of consensus politics that is normal in most democratic societies.'

The newspapers became forums for debate, with Collins and Martin leading their respective communities in the new politics. Joint editorials demonstrated that two papers with deep-seated political differences could unite around certain fundamentals – such as opposition to violence and support for peace – in support of the peace process.

Collins and Martin received awards for their contribution to press freedom by highlighting the role the print media can play in fostering democratic practices. This is in stark contrast to the media in other parts of the world: in former Yugoslavia and Rwanda, for instance, the media played a key role in fomenting hatred.

Not all newspapers were able to come out as firmly as the *News Letter*, the *Irish News* and the *Belfast Telegraph*. While it was easier for nationalist newspapers to support the process in its entirety, for some Unionist newspapers, whose readers were split between those favouring the agreement and those opposing, survival meant hedging their bets or giving a subliminal message rather than an overt one. Ulster Unionist leader David Trimble, who, of course, supported the agreement, was portrayed in profiles and features as brave and willing to take risks. His picture appeared above the fold, with the main opposition leaders, the Rev Ian Paisley or the leader of the UK Unionists, Bob McCartney, appearing lower down or on a left-hand inside page. Such layout tricks indicated how editors were thinking and obviated the need for editorial comment. Drumcree, they said, showed how fragile the peace was and how difficult it was for local newspapers to reflect their own divided communities.

Northern Ireland's newspapers are in a state of flux in a media market that is increasingly seen as one market for the whole island, even the two islands. The successful family-owned *Derry Journal* has just been bought by the Mirror Group for £18.25 million (US$28 million). It is now an uneasy stable mate of the unionist *News Letter*. The *News Letter*'s newsroom is a strange sight indeed: seated before their computer terminals at one end of the room are the journalists writing for the traditional voice of Ulster unionism; at the other, are the *Mirror* journalists, writing for the Irish edition of a newspaper that once called for 'Troops Out'.

The *Belfast Telegraph* is now owned by Trinity Holdings, making it simply a part of that company's empire of 120 regional and local newspapers in the UK. Trinity also owns the Dublin-based *Sunday Business Post*. Scottish Radio Holdings has an increasing powerful media presence in Northern Ireland.

But if Northern Ireland's media is becoming little more than outposts of British media empires, some things will always remind media executives that Northern Ireland still has its own rules. Last May, days before the Referendum, BBC Radio Foyle hosted a debate broadcast over the Radio Ulster network.

According to the head of Radio Foyle, Anna Leddy, provision had to be made for those who would not share a platform. While the debate took place in a university lecture theatre in front of an invited audience, two separate studios were set up for those unwilling to appear on the main platform with their opponents. ❏

MF

RICHARD KEARNEY

Beyond sovereignty

Dual identity, joint sovereignty, the spread of regional and supranational entities and the end of the nation state as we know it... The Good Friday Agreement makes a nonsense of warring nationalities and begs us to reconsider the notion of exclusive territorial sovereignty

One of the most innovative proposals of the Good Friday Agreement of April 1998 is the new 'Council of Isles'. What this effectively acknowledges is that the citizens of Britain and Ireland are inextricably bound up with each other – mongrel islanders from east to west sharing an increasingly common civic and economic space. In addition to the obvious contemporary overlapping of our sports and popular cultures, it is worth recalling just how much of our respective histories were shared, from the Celtic, Viking and Norman settlements to our more recent entry into the European community. For millennia, the Irish sea served as a waterway connecting our two islands, only rarely as a *cordon sanitaire* separating our peoples. It is not surprising that over eight million citizens of the UK today claim Irish origin; while, as is well known, almost a quarter of the inhabitants of the island of Ireland claim to be British.

The Good Friday Agreement acknowledges the right of Northern Irelanders to a dual identity. After the joint referenda north and south of the border in May 1998, any of its citizens can now legitimately claim to be 'British or Irish or both' (page 2, para vi). The 'both' is crucial here, in that it allows, for the first time in Anglo-Irish history, the declaration of a double allegiance to Irish and British sovereignty. This means (though no-one is shouting about it) that a practical form of joint sovereignty has been endorsed by the great majority of the Irish electorate, in addition to the near-unanimous ratification by the British parliamentary parties in Westminster.

The pluralisation of national identity epitomised by the provision of a Council of Isles is due acknowledgment of the centrality of east-west relations, and entails a radical redefinition of the hallowed notion of sovereignty. In essence, it means the 'deterritorialisation' of national sovereignty and the attribution of sovereignty to people rather than to land. A fact that finds a symbolic corollary in the extension of national 'belonging' to embrace the Irish diaspora now numbering over 70 million worldwide.

The new Agreement marks a shift in the traditional understanding of sovereignty as previously inscribed in the exclusivist territorial claims of successive British governments and the Irish constitution. The change in articles 2 and 3 of the Irish Constitution and the British Government of Ireland Act is far more portentious than most commentators have realised.

What it amounts to is a revolution in our thinking about sovereignty. The term sovereignty originally referred to the supreme power of a divine ruler; only later was it delegated to divinely elected 'representatives' in this world – to kings, pontiffs, emperors, monarchs – and, finally, to the 'people' in most modern states. A problem arose, however, in that many modern democracies recognize the existence of several different peoples within a single state. And many peoples means many centres of sovereignty. Yet the tradional concept of sovereignty was always unitary, 'one and indivisible'. Whence the dilemma: how to divide the indivisible?

This is why, today, sovereignty has become one of the most controversial concepts in political theory and international law, intimately related to issues of state government, national independence and minority rights. Inherited notions of absolutist sovereignty are now being challenged both from within nation states and by developments in international legislation. With the Hague Conferences of 1899 and 1907, followed by the Covenant of the League of Nations and the Charter of the UN, significant restrictions on the actions of nation states were laid down. A system of international checks and balances was introduced limiting the right of sovereign states to act as they pleased in all matters. Moreover, the increasing interdependence of states – accompanied by a sharing of sovereignties in the interests of greater peace, social justice and economic exchange – qualifies the very principle of absolute sovereignty. As the *Encyclopaedia Britannica* puts it:

'The people of the world have recognised that there can be no peace without law, and that there can be no law without some limitations on sovereignty. They have started, therefore, to pool sovereignties to the extent needed to maintain peace; and sovereignty is being increasingly exercised on behalf of the peoples of the world not only by national governments but also by organisations of the world community'.

If this pertains to the 'peoples of the world' generally, how much more does in pertain to the peoples of the islands of Britain and Ireland? In *Post Nationalist Ireland* published in 1997, I argued for a surpassing of the existing nation-states in the direction of both an Irish-British Council and a federal Europe of regions. The nation-state has become both too large and too small as a model of contemporary government. Too large for the growing needs of regional participatory democracy; too small for the increasing drift toward transnational exchange and power-sharing. Hence my invocation of the Nordic Council as a model for resolving our sovereignty disputes, in particular the way in which these five nation states and three autonomous regions succeeded in sorting out territorial conflicts, declaring the Aland and Spitsbergen islands as Europe's first two demilitarised zones. Might we not do likewise under the aegis of a new transnational British-Irish Council, declaring Northern Ireland a third demilitarised zone?

To date, such sovereignty sharing has been opposed by British nationalism. It is, ironically, the Irish republican tradition (which comprises all democratic parties in the Irish Republic as well as the SDLP and Sinn Féin in the North) which is usually labelled 'nationalist', even though the most uncompromising nationalists in the whole sorry business of Northern Ireland have been the Unionists. It was the Unionists, after all, who clung to the outdated notion of undiluted British sovereignty, refusing any compromise with their Irish neighbours, until Tony Blair blew the whistle and Trimble trembled and turned. John Hume's 'new republicanism' – a vision of shared sovereignty between the different peoples of this island – had little difficulty with the new 'post-nationalist' scenario. Indeed, Hume called himself a 'post-nationalist' for many years witout many taking heed.

The real threat posed by the post-nationalist scenario is to traditional Unionism, as the June Assembly elections proved. Deprived of the shield of Thatcherism, the Unionists of Ulster had to face the tune of a new future and accept the inevitability of sovereignty sharing in both north-south and east-west directions. They could no longer march to the tribal anthem of a people apart in a place apart.

That the British government under Tony Blair was prepared to grasp the sovereignty nettle and acknowledge the ineluctability of the break-up of Britain, is to its credit. But it was not an action *ex nihilo*. There were precedents for sovereignty sharing and shearing in Britain's recent experience, albeit not always highlighted. These would have included Britain's consent to a limitation and dilution of sovereign national power in its subscription to the European Convention on Human Rights, the Single European Act, the European Common Defence Policy and the European Court of Justice. If Britain had been able to pool sovereignty in these ways with the other nation-states of the EU, surely it is logical to do with its closest neighbour, the Irish Republic. Moreover, the EU principles of subsidiarity and of local democracy, promoted in the European Charter of Self-Government, offers a real alternative to the clash of British-Irish nationalisms that has paralysed Northern Ireland for decades.

The implications of the Good Friday Agreement are obvious: the conflict of sovereignty claims exercised over the same territory by two independent governments and the ensuing decades of violence, is now being superseded by a postnationalist paradigm of intergovernmental power. The multiple identities of Northern Ireland have always belied the feasibility of 'unitary' forms of goverment, be it a United Kingdom or a United Ireland. Hence the wisdom of separating the notion of nation (identity) from that of state (sovereignty) thereby allowing the co-existence of different communities in the same society; and, by extension, amplifying the models of national identification to include more pluralist forms of association – a British-Irish council, a European network of regions, and the Irish and British disasporas.

The fact is, as the Agreement recognizes, there are no pristine nations around which definitive state boundaries – demarcating exclusivist sovereignty status – can be established. Germany's attempts to do this from Bismark to Hitler led to successive wars. It also recognizes the historic futility of both British and Irish constitutional claims on Northen Ireland as a natural and necessary part of their respective 'national territories'.

The Council of Isles ultimately promises a network of interconnecting regional assemblies guaranteeing parity of esteem for cultural and political diversity. The challenge is surely to abandon our mutual reinforcing myths of superiority (largely British) and purity (largely Irish) and face our more mundane post-imperial, post-nationalist reality. Could it not, as Simon Partridge argues, even be an inspiration to other parts of Europe and the globe so hopelessly enmired in the devastations of exclusive ethnic nationalism?

The first Irish character in English literature, Captain Macmorris of Shakespeare's *Henry V*, asks the question: 'What is my nation?' This quest for national identity has not gone away. Nor should it. What the new Agreement allows is that such a quest be gradually channelled away from the fetish of the nation-state, where history has shown its tenure to be insecure and belligerent, to more appropriate levels of regional and federal expression. In the Irish-British context, this means that citizens of these islands can come to express their identity less in terms of rival sovereign states and more in terms of locally empowered provinces – Ulster, Scotland, Wales, etc – and larger international associations – the British-Irish Council and the European Union. The new dispensation fosters multiple layers of compatible identification - regional, national and transnational. It allows anyone in Northern Ireland to declare her/himself a citizen of the Ulster region, the Irish and/or British nation, the European Community and, in the widest sense, the cosmopolitan order of world citizenry.

Citizens of these islands might do better to think of themselves as 'mongrel islanders' than as dwellers of two pure, god-given nation states. These is no such thing as primordial nationality. Every nation is a hybrid construct, an 'imagined community' that can be re-imagined again in alternative versions. The challenge is to embrace this process of hybridisation from which we derive and to which we are committed willy-nilly. In the face of resurgent nationalisms in these islands and elsewhere, fired by rhetorics of purity and purification, we do well to remember that we are all mongrelised, interdependent, mixed-up.

Richard Kearney is a professor of philosophy at University College Dublin. He is the author of many works of philosophy and two novels. His most recent work is Post Nationalist Ireland

MICHAEL FOLEY

One law for all

Alongside the high profile provisions of the Belfast Agreement – the Assembly, elections, devolved government and the north-south institutions – there are others that have scarcely figured in post-Agreement debate, in particular the creation of human rights commission for north as well as south

The Agreement says that a Human Rights Commission will be set up and that the Irish government will also establish a Human Rights Commission 'with a mandate and remit equivalent to that within Northern Ireland'. The history of the past 25 years and longer leaves few in any doubt that an independent body with strong powers is necessary to protect human rights in Northern Ireland.

The wording might lead one to suppose that the only reason for the Irish government to be bound by a similar provision is simply to show willing: its human rights record is far better than that in the north and the Republic's constitutions offers a degree of protection that has never been available in Northern Ireland. But there is also a sneaking feeling that the provision of a Human Rights Commission in the South became part of the agreement because it would have been impossible for Dublin to demand the establishment of bodies ensuring human rights for those living in the north without a similar standard for its own citizens.

However, with the decision to incorporate into British law the European Convention on Human Rights, and the statements by the Irish *Taoiseach* (Prime Minister) Bertie Ahern that this will not take place in the south (*Index* 2/1998), it appears that citizens of the north will have a greater degree of rights protection than those in the Republic.

Human rights commissions are not an invention of the peace process; they were first suggested as far back as 1946. In 1991, the Paris Principles drawn up by the UN Commission on Human Rights, laid down guidelines for national human rights commissions. Such bodies, they said, would examine legislation and proposed legislation to ensure compatibility with international human rights standards as well as investigate human rights violations and raise awareness of human rights.

Northern Ireland has had its Standing Advisory Commission on Human Rights (SACHR) since 1973. Its legal officer, Denise Magill, speaking at a conference organised by the Irish Council for Civil Liberties (ICCL) and the Committee for the Administration of Justice in Dublin this year, welcomed the new Commission and said it must have just such a broad mandate, necessary in a society emerging from conflict.

The new body, which will replace SACHR, will indeed have a wider remit and greater powers than the latter. The Agreement provides the new Commission with a legal basis and empowers it to:

● review the adequacy and effectiveness of laws and practices;
● make recommendations to government;
● provide information and promote awareness of human rights;
● consider draft legislation;
● institute legal proceedings or provide assistance to those who wish to do so;
● consult and advise on the scope for defining, in UK legislation, rights supplementary to those in the European Convention on Human Rights;
● establish a joint committee with the new Irish Human Rights Commission as a forum for looking at human rights issues on the island as a whole.

If it is allowed to function effectively, the new Commission will be of immense importance to Northern Ireland, not least in helping to draft a Bill of Rights. It will be involved in formulating those rights such as cultural rights and parity of esteem not included in the ECHR. It will also have to take a general position on issues specific to Northern Ireland, such as finding the balance between the rights of marchers to freedom of assembly alongside the right of residents to freedom of movement or freedom to live without harassment.

Human rights commissions are not only for societies emerging from years of violent conflict: they exist in Australia, New Zealand, India and South Africa and are being actively promoted within the Commonwealth. They are now a major factor in the UN's strategy to establish widely accepted international human rights standards that are implemented by member states.

The decision to include the Human Rights Commissions in the Belfast Agreement could have two interesting and far reaching consequences. In the first instance, the Irish Republic's Commission is a gift not to be wasted, something that could happen only too easily given the reluctance of the Irish government to consider incorporating the ECHR into Irish law. At the June conference in Dublin, joint chairman of the ICCL Michael Farrell said, 'The rather off-hand way the proposed Human Rights Commission for the Republic is dealt with in the Good Friday Agreement, and the lack of prior discussion and consultation about its establishment gives rise to concern that the Irish government envisages it as a fairly token body to be set up for reasons of political symmetry with the new institution in Northern Ireland. That would fly in the face of the intentions of the Paris Principles and the subsequent UN resolutions and the declaration on national institutions, including the most recent one co-sponsored by Ireland at the UN Human Rights Commission session in last April.'

'It would also squander an opportunity to develop a culture of human rights and to establish a credible mechanism for dealing with rights-based grievances at a time when our society is changing rapidly and becoming more diverse, more multi-cultural and more divided.'

But there is another. Citizens in other parts of the UK might wonder why they have less rights protection than those living in Northern Ireland. If only one Commission is established in the UK, that in Northern Ireland, the message will be clear: this was necessary because of the peculiar circumstances of Northern Ireland. The inclusion of the Republic changes that. Professor Brice Dickson of the University of Ulster, author of *Creating an Effective Human Rights Commission for Northern Ireland*, argues that by singling out Northern Ireland and rejecting a human rights commission for the UK, those of a predominantly British identity in Northern Ireland may be alienated from the Commission, which will, at the same time, raise the expectations of advocates of human rights commissions elsewhere. If the new Scottish and Welsh parliaments decide to create their own commissions, England could find itself the only part of these islands without such a level of human rights protection. ❏

MF

MAIRTIN CRAWFORD

Belfast speaks

A staunch republican from west Belfast, Joe, (not his real name) voted 'Yes' in the Referendum, and has faith that the Sinn Fein leadership can deliver. After the Omagh atrocity he was direct in his condemnation.
'The people who did this aren't republicans. What are they achieving? Nothing. They have nothing to offer. This guy, the quartermaster (who defected from the IRA earlier this year to join the so-called 'Real IRA'), is an out of control fanatic. Some people are saying the the Provies should sort them out, nut them, take them out of operation, but there is always a danger that this may cause a feud. It's happened before. The bomb in Omagh was extremely depressing. After all the gains made through politics these idiots are trying to wreck things. But I don't think they'll succeed. They have no real support and the Omagh thing has effectively made them outcasts, even in hard-core republican areas. Politics, not violence, is the way forward now.'

A catholic, and single mother of three living in the tiny nationalist enclave on Belfast's lower Ormeau Road, Siobhan is hesitantly optimistic about the future.
'While I am hopeful about the prospects of peace in the long term I wouldn't want my children to grow up here if things got bad again. That was a terrible thing that happened in Omagh, so much needless suffering. If that sort of thing was going on, if things went back to the way they were before the ceasefires, I would leave. Definitely. I would emigrate. I have relatives in Canada so I might go there if I could get a visa. Or England maybe. There has been trouble in the area I live in – the Orangemen march past our street each year. They are not wanted but they do it anyway. Two years ago we were curfewed by the RUC and not allowed out for 24 hours. It was a disgrace. It's terrible for the kids to be exposed to this. After all, they're the future. I had hoped that the Agreement and the referendum and all that would have changed things. But there are bad people on

both sides who don't want change.'

Judy has just arrived in Belfast from New York to spend a year studying for an MA in Irish Studies at a local university.

'I came to Belfast to study because I'm interested in Irish history, specifically the political situation here, in the north. When I first started getting interested in here it was when the ceasefires were being announced, but I think I would have come if there hadn't been a process. But the peace process certainly helped. The bomb in Omagh was really unsettling but I don't think it will make me want to leave. If things got really bad, like before the ceasefires, I might think about leaving then. I would probably think about it but I don't know if I would go. In America the news the people have been getting about the Agreement and that has all come across as good news. Americans are very confused about events like Drumcree because it seems that things haven't changed. And then the bomb in Omagh, I would assume, would just confirm that; make people think that things haven't really changed at all.'

Avril, a 31-year-old business professional, is originally from Dublin. She lived in various parts of England for 10 years before moving to Belfast last September to start a new job.

'Having left Dublin to live and work in several cities in England and Scotland, I found that integration as a citizen was possible because of an increasing acceptance and accommodation of diverse cultures and identities. The people of Northern Ireland should not be afraid of difference. I relocated to Belfast in anticipation that the prospects for the economy in the north would improve and opportunities increase. Without the implementation of the Good Friday Agreement the prospects for this will be delayed and it's unlikely that I would be prepared to invest time and energy here under such uncertain circumstances. I'd like to spend more time here – the vibrancy and character of this place and the Irish personality is very evident wherever I go, despite all the stories of loss and adversity. I don't think the spirit of the Irish people will ever be broken, but the devastation in Omagh will leave another scar on the psyche of the Irish people that can never heal completely.' ❏

Mairtin Crawford is production editor for Fortnight

Evening (for peace)

I

Out after work into a three-day freeze,
official winter time's precocious dark descending;
by the city walls the wind whips
my face raw, while on shaded ledges
patches of morning frost still nibble on stone.
'Official' winter-time' – it suggests decision,
the toss between going out in the first streaks of morning
or coming back as darkness falls.
Reason votes for the rhythm of the farm,
the children safe from harm;
Can we make the new Ulster so dispassionately,
and through a white cloth of tolerance
sift and strain the hard edges of identity?

2

Out after work into the same streets
as the evening the siege was lifted
a mere four lifetimes end to end ago;
this selfsame wind has rubbed their ancient
names from the tombstones in the churchyard,
worn the cobbles three times down to dust.
But the besieged feelings, fed on
ritual and story, fuel a hungry flame.
Ritual invaders become the familiar enemies
from the next street, the different religion;
needing real sacrifices, pageant begets
persecution, and Lundy's burning effigy
consumes the city's peace (even victorious
swords have two edges; but sharper
than any sword, Lord, spare us the bitter word).

Amen ❑

*Jack Houlahan, poet and playwright, lives and works in Derry where he is
acting director of Northlands, an alcohol and drug agency. The above excerpt is
from* A Londonderry Prayer, *winner of the 1998 Derry City Council
competition 'The human right thing to do'*

Wear the chador on the inside

Jame'eh-ye Salem, one of Iran's more outspoken publications and, unusually, edited by a woman, invited a group of teenagers – boys as well as girls – to express their views on matters of concern to them. They spoke of an educational system that was failing them, the wearing of the chador and the segregation of the sexes. The girls spoke of their passion for football and fashion

Jame'eh-ye Salem: Almost 70 per cent of Iran's population is under 20 years of age. So we have invited you to our offices to listen to your problems and questions. Don't hesitate to speak freely.

Golbahar: I was really happy to take part in the presidential election last year [23 May 1997 in which Mohammad Khatami was elected]. At last we had the feeling that someone was listening to us. Let me start by talking about our educational system: its methods are antiquated and irrelevant. Pupils really don't want to attend classes. Our teachers are boring and frequently useless. We are part of a new generation; they should find new ways of teaching us, ways that are more suited to the times we're living in now. They should do something that encourages people to go to school rather than leaving us with the feeling that what we are being taught is outmoded and irrelevant to our lives.

Ramine: The main problem is that we only work to get good marks so that when our fathers come home in the evening they praise us and encourage us; so that we are given a present; or even so that our parents

Credit: Barth/Rex

can boast of our achievements to the rest of the family. But if our teachers tried to be in touch with the real problems that concern us and allowed us to participate actively in talking about these, we would feel that we had some involvement with the way our society is developing. If that happened, it's more than likely that sooner or later we, this country, would be able to shake off this 'Third World' label. It carries the implication that we are somehow intellectually 'retarded'.

Nazanine: Another problem is that we have this tendency to fake it: we express ourselves in an over-demonstrative, exaggerated way and pretend to believe things we really don't believe in at all. For instance, if a teacher wants to get a job in the state education system she wears the chador. This particular practice should disappear. It ends up producing exactly the opposite effect to that desired: it makes us deaf to what they are trying to inculcate in us.

Nargues: It's true. Those who act in this shallow way do no service to the very values they claim to be promoting – this goes as much for secular values as for religious.

Nazanine: As to the chador: some schools insist on girls wearing it as opposed to the headscarf even though there is no law on this. However, I have to say that the wearing of the chador is only one aspect of our problems, not the be all and end all.

Golbahar: In the first place, faith must be deep and internal. One has to believe in what one does. A woman should wear her veil internally, not on the outside. Being forced to wear it for public consumption has nothing to do with her personal conviction. It may even encourage a lack of conviction. In a way, it forces her to lie. Things should be done so that students can carry out their religious obligations with belief in them and because they feel the need.

Ramine: When we have tests on religion, the teachers go into everything in such minute detail that we very quickly switch off. Our society is very suspicious of young people, particularly when they're unmarried.

Nazanine: Just a little while ago, the authorities once again segregated boys and girls at the university. Is there any valid reason for this? Even when they're of marriagable age they keep them apart. Young people must be able to meet normally somewhere; one of these days they going to get married and will have to set up life together. But we are segregated at school, at university and we can't even be seen together in the streets. No wonder the divorce rate is rising: how can a couple stay together when the husband and wife, have never been given the chance to get to know one another.

Ramine: They think fashion is a curse, a plague. Young people are harassed and under pressure all the time because of fashion. Every time a new trend gets taken up, they warn us that those who follow it will be punished. It would be better to forbid the promotion of a particular fashion rather than to threaten those who take it up.

Golbahar: Well I personally can't see how following a particular fashion can become tantamount to breaking the law. How can a fashion be OK in one place and evil in another?

Ramine: They keep on telling us, over and over again, not to veer towards the West. How can we ignore what we hear on radio and television about its progress in science, technology, medicine? We need this sort of information if we are to understand the world around us. We can't simply reject everything in western culture. For instance, thousands of Iranians have a passion for football. The big stadium in western Tehran is reserved exclusively for men. What are the women who love football supposed to do? Why can't girls watch football? Why don't they tell us the reasons behind this ban? No-one has ever tried to organise a round table so that we can talk about our claims; so that they can listen and make some effort to understand us.

JS: The authorities today are asking you to come forward and express your views on the mistakes they've made as far as you are concerned.

Golbahar: But who are we supposed to talk to? This magazine has asked for our views, but that's still pretty unusual. Most of the time we have the feeling our words fall on deaf ears: no-one deigns to listen to our views. ❏

From Jame'eh-ye Salem *(A Healthy Society)*. *Translated from* Courrier International *by Judith Vidal-Hall*

What the parents say

A number of newspapers have been conducting opinion polls among their readers on the burning political issues of the day. *Doniya-ye Sokhan* (The World of Words, a literary monthly) was particularly interested in their views on the President and relations with the USA; *Kar va Kargar* (Work and the Worker, a left-wing Muslim daily) questioned them on unemployment and the cost of living; *Azadi* (Freedom, a pro-democracy Muslim weekly) asked them to define 'civil society'.

Mr Jafari, researcher: Just like Gandhi, Mr Khatami is the sort of President you'll find queuing alongside you at the bakers. Why? Because he is thoroughly sincere. What he is doing culturally is a good example: he kicked off a real renaissance. Since his victory at the polls, there has been a spectacular boom in the book market. Works that were at one time banned are now being published.

Miss Sharaji, communications student: Our President finds it difficult to do the things he wants to because of the commanding positions his rivals occupy in the state structure. This reinforces the position of the speaker of the majlis, Nategh Nuri [Khatami's defeated conservative rival in the 1997 presidential election] and cripples his minority government. As a result, after the conservatives criticised his highly successful interview with CNN, Mr Khatami suddenly hardened his tone towards the USA. Sure, newspapers have much greater freedom of expression, but censorship, particularly of the TV, is still around.

Mrs Razeghi, office worker: The housing shortage is basically a result of the black market and the proliferation of middlemen or agents who totally lack scruples. Rents are prohibitive. The government should embark on a massive public-housing scheme and provide low-interest mortgages so that ordinary people can buy them.

Miss Mohammadi, student: The price of books and texts goes up daily. Bookshops are poor. During his election campaign, the President repeatedly said he would help the young people of this country. All we ask is that he keeps his promises.

Mr Karami, salesman: The price hike is out of control. If it wants to ease the economic pressure of daily living that is grinding people down, the government should deal with the middlemen who are at the root of this. Goods should be sold at fixed prices, in the same way as books.

Mr Ahmadi, worker: Every single day we workers confront the most appalling economic dificulties: lack of housing, salary cuts and so on. There is too much injustice in Iran. We demand of the President that he pay serious attention to this.

Mr Akbari, butcher: Civil society means justice. Mr Rafsanjani's government wasn't too bad but, in the end, it was the rich who profited from it.

Mr Mohammadi, teacher: Forget all the fine words. Civil society is nothing more or less than a true Islamic society: an egalitarian society without a class system.

Miss Alizadeh, graphic designer: There would be nothing particularly different about a civil society except that the state would abandon its interventionist role and become an observer, alongside the people rather than superior to them. To establish such a society would mean fundamental changes in our constitution and much more seriously implemented laws, particularly the legislation that concern the rights of women. ❏

EDWARD LUCIE-SMITH

Letter from Pärnu

The Pärnu International Documentary and Anthropology Film Festival in Estonia had some suprises in store, including the breaking of some long held taboos

Documentary films are one of the ways in which the smaller nations of the world assert their identity. Chairing the jury at the 12th Annual Pärnu International Documentary and Anthropology Film Festival (to give it its full title) was an eye-opener in more ways than one.

Pärnu is a small, sleepy seaside resort in Estonia, about one-and-a-half hours by road from the capital, Tallinn. As its title implies, the festival was already in existence during the communist period, but has now become one of the symbols of Estonia's newly regained political independence. It even, as the minister of culture reminded us at the closing ceremony, gets a special budget of its own from the government.

In his touchingly idealistic introductory statement printed in the festival brochure, Mark Soosaar, the director of the festival, made it clear that this was an occasion with strong moral overtones. His wishes for himself and his colleagues he said, were to 'try to understand and believe those people whose lives we are hoisting up on the screen more. That way we can manage to look more deeply into the soul of our own people'.

Because the festival is located where it is, it seemed natural to find a substantial number of films from the four Baltic republics – Finland, Estonia, Lithuania and Latvia – plus others from Russia, Romania, Poland and Hungary. These were, not surprisingly, the contributions with the greatest degree of political resonance for the western viewer, and one or two touched directly on current political problems.

The film with perhaps the sharpest political impact came from Latvia, where post-communist political tensions are currently severe. Entitled *Is*

It Easy to Be..., it was a sequel to a famous documentary made in Latvia right at the end of the Soviet period. This examined the attitudes of the increasingly westernised young, their passion for western fashions and western rock music, their impassioned rejection of the leaden dreariness of communism. The Soviet authorities resisted showing this film almost to the last ditch and, when it was finally released, there were long queues to see it, not merely in Latvia itself but all over the Soviet Union. The decision to show it marked a significant breach in the established system of censorship, and was one of the landmarks on the road to the dissolution of the communist regime itself.

Children of Gaia (Gaias børn) - Credit: Bente Milton

The film-maker responsible for the original documentary, Juris Podnieks, is now dead, but a decade later, one of his assistants, Antra Clinska, had the idea of trying to trace the young people featured in the film to find out what had happened to them. The message she brought back was not a comforting one. The only person who seemed reasonably happy with the way things had gone was a complacent young materialist who, having announced his wish to possess all the glittering toys capitalism could offer, had fulfilled most of his ambitions by moving to London and going to work for one of the UK's great accountancy firms, Coopers & Lybrand. The rest were largely disillusioned. One was dead – a suicide. Another, with her husband's knowledge and consent, was working as a prostitute on the streets of Riga. While it seems unlikely that this sequel will be as widely seen as its predecessor, those who do see it will find it hard to maintain much optimism about the state of post-communist society in Latvia.

'it did not make things much better that this self-censorship seemed to be largely unconscious'

Another film which used a rather similar structure was a Finnish documentary called *Anna*. Here the central figure was a Siberian woman from the minority Nganasan people who, as a child, had featured in one of those optimistic Soviet films about how every day in every way things were getting better and better. Later she had risen to be secretary of her local branch of the Communist Party. The film was basically a record of her terrible disillusionment and of the degradation that had overtaken her people as a result of Soviet policies.

Is It Easy to Be... was at any rate a film that spoke its mind. Other post-communist films were unintentionally rather than intentionally disturbing because of their hints, and sometimes more than hints, of self-censorship. It did not make things much better that this self-censorship seemed to be largely unconscious.

In order to explain this more fully one has to look briefly at the history of the Pärnu Festival itself. Its bias from the beginning has been anthropological, and in Estonia, as in other non-Russian territories forcibly attached to, or at any rate dominated by, the Soviet Union, this seems to have been interpreted in a special way. The business of the anthropological film was not simply to record, but actually to help to preserve, the traditions of minority peoples. It is not accidental that

Pärnu offers a special prize for 'a film about survival'.

In the Soviet period, there was a fashion in the Baltic territories for documentary films, slow but beautifully made, recording rural customs and the 'traditional' way of life of various ethnic minorities. The festival demonstrated that this still survives very strongly in Lithuania. A small group of beautifully made but also slightly vacuous films in black and white showed that time had apparently stood still for the documentarists who work there. None offered a glimpse of contemporary urban life in their country. Rather similar attitudes surfaced in a visually very seductive colour film about gypsies, made near Kazan by the Russian

Children of Gaia (Gaias børn) - Credit: Bente Milton

director Marina Razbeshkina. Concentrating on a time of Christmas celebration, *Inheritors of Heaven* had a dreamy detachment from the political and social implications of what was being recorded which left a slightly disturbing aftertaste. Its subjects were treated like the exotic inhabitants of an aquarium full of tropical fish.

An out-of-competition film - one of the few I had time to see - used some of the conventions of the category I have just been describing, but broke ranks with the complacency which typified it. Called *Dog Trails*, and made by a Finnish director, it was a portrait of a Russian Karelian woodsman living near the Finnish border, who had been forced to serve in opposing armies during World War II, and who had then been rewarded with a 10-year sentence in a Russian prison camp which destroyed his marriage and left a legacy of family bitterness. History has left the Baltic region with many sore places, moral and physical, even if the makers of documentaries are sometimes humanly reluctant to acknowledge this fact.

Of course, the Pärnu Festival had much more to offer than films from Russia and from formerly communist territories; in fact, only one of the major prize-winners came from this orbit − a piece about a pair of Romanian street kids and their baby made by a Belgian studio. This, which won the 'survival' category, could, I suppose be thought of as a post-Ceaucescu film, since the social conditions it depicted are a direct legacy of the Ceaucescu dictatorship. Basically, however, it was a gripping narrative about imperfect but courageous people struggling for existence. One indication of the director's intentions was that she tended to film her subjects in very tight close-up: background details were dismissed as irrelevant. Though one knew that the events were real, and that what was said and done was unscripted, it had a close − perhaps too close − affinity to the methods of fiction.

The outright winner, from Denmark, was an astonishing film about our attitudes to the physically handicapped. *Gaia's Children* was directed by yet another woman director, Bente Milton, and posed uncomfortable questions. For example, why do we admire the Venus de Milo when we can hardly bear to look at a living woman who has been born without arms? These queries acquired additional force because the narrator − also partly responsible for the script − was the footless British actor Nabil Shaban. Here, I think, one encounters what is really the final question about censorship and the cinema. It's not merely a matter of what the political authorities suppress, because for one reason or another they don't want us to know about it. Or even about what film-makers consciously or unconsciously omit, because it doesn't suit their point of view. It's also about what we ourselves are willing to look at – and how we construe what we see. ❏

Edward Lucie-Smith *is a writer and art critic. He has two books appearing shortly:* Adam, a consideration of the male nude in art *(Weidenfeld/Rizzoli) and* Zoo, images of animals *(Watson-Guptill). He is currently working on* Images of Women in Art *in collaboration with Judy Chicago*

RUSSELL BAIRD TEWKSBURY

Cache 22

A technical 'fix' to speed-up data transfers could result in an irreversible loss of free expression on the Internet

With each passing day, the Internet is expanding and becoming more congested. It is estimated that at the end of August 1998 the Internet consisted of more than 140,000 networks, connecting more than 130 million users worldwide. With the massive expansion over the last three years, Internet traffic jams and bottlenecks, or what are known as flashpoints and hot-spots, have become daily occurrences. Network administrators are faced with the difficult challenge of how to provide more efficient bandwidth and server utilisation to their customers. In order to meet that challenge, many are turning to 'proxy caching' as a solution.

Client-side caching occurs as Internet users surf the Web. Client-side refers to everything on the user's side of the modem link, server-side to the world out there beyond your desktop. Each web page a user visits is cached – copied and stored – on the user's desktop machine. When that same user wishes to load a previously visited web document, the user's computer first looks for the cached copy before going back to the original source. On the network side, a similar duplication process occurs: this is proxy caching and is performed automatically by the server software. Proxy caching results in countless digital duplicates or clones of original web pages being saved, then served, on many different networks throughout the Internet. Network users receive web documents saved on the local server rather than the source server. In short, an original web page is redistributed many times over by someone other than the original content provider or copyright holder.

To facilitate this process, the development of an international hierarchical cache system, or global mesh, is well under way. These cache systems are being designed to be interconnected to the national backbone networks, thereby creating a worldwide caching infrastructure. Some of the many web cache projects under way include NLANR – National Laboratory for Applied Network Research (USA); CHOC – Project (Europe); JANET – National Web Cache (UK); NZIX – New Zealand Internet Exchange-Cache (New Zealand); W3 CACHE (Poland); STIX – SingNet Hierarchical Cache Proxy (Singapore); CINECA – (Italy); Japan Cache (Japan). As the Internet evolves into this international global mesh of caches, its formerly decentralised architecture will become centralised around these cache clearing houses, providing far fewer points of access to the network.

Both proxy caching and impending implementation of an international hierarchical cache system set the stage for abuses such as individual monitoring and surveillance, tampering, identity theft, censorship, intellectual property or copyright infringement, invasion of privacy, and taxation by government. The integrity of information will decline and data security risks are sure to escalate.

Proxy caching is not yet as common a practice in the USA as it is in places such as Japan and Europe, where bandwidth is more expensive and restrictions to it are more common. Among many network administrators, the prevailing attitude is that proxy caching is a good thing. For example, Cache Now! is an Internet-based campaign designed to 'increase the awareness and use of proxy caching on the Web. Web cache offers a win/win situation for both content providers and users.' In the USA, NLANR is working on a cache project entitled 'A Distributed Testbed for National Information Provisioning'. According to NLANR, the goal of the project is 'to facilitate the evolution of an efficient national architecture for handling highly popular information'. NLANR submitted a proposal to the National Science Foundation entitled 'A Distributed Architecture for Global WWW Cache Integration'. It stated, 'What is needed is an information provisioning architecture to support efficient information distribution through the widespread use of network-adaptive caching.'

NLANR's report also states the disadvantages of network caching: 'Information providers lose access counts on their servers. Occasionally non-transparent to end users. Often requires manual configuration. There is always a finite chance of receiving stale data. Requires additional resources (hardware, personnel). Can be a single point of failure. And depending on your point of view, caching has these features which generally find favour among administrators and managers, but are unwelcomed by users: Hides true client address. Provides an opportunity

'hierarchical cache systems set the stage for abuses such as individual monitoring and surveillance, identity theft, censorship'

to analyse and monitor user's activities. *Can be used to block access to certain sites'*. [Emphasis added]

Both Cache Now and the National Laboratory for Applied Network Research declined to be interviewed for this article. However, NLANR has indirectly addressed some of the same issues on its web site. Buried deep within NLANR's web site one will find their statement regarding statistics collection which includes the following: 'Of even greater concern may be the possible misuse of cached statistical data. Information privacy policies built into the structure of originating web sites mean nothing if intermediate caches have sole control of access data. This may include sensitive information about sites and users viewing those pages and selecting particular links. Is the caching organisation free to do whatever it wants with that information? Sell it for marketing lists? Provide it for investigative purposes as they see fit? Sell it to commercial databases? An original web site may have strict policies on information collected from users visiting their web server. But a cache may have a completely different policy, or none at all.'

The potential for problems with numerous networks having countless copies of other people's web pages is a content provider's worst nightmare: loss of control. There is no independent mechanism or standard in place for knowing who has cached a copy of a web page, whether it is a current version, or whether it's been altered in any way. Every piece of software monitoring traffic – used for justifying advertising rates charged to web page sponsors – is essentially rendered ineffective: the more popular a particular web page is, the more times it will be cached. For content providers whose business is based on generating advertising revenue, proxy caching reduces the number of reported page views to a given web site; advertising revenue is thus more difficult to substantiate.

Further, there is the problem of how to maintain consistency or freshness of content on a page that has been cached. As an original web page changes or updates, every cached copy must be updated or it becomes outdated. In addition, the recent proliferation of dynamically created web pages makes it even harder to implement caches. The current solution is for the cache owner – not the content provider – to choose how fresh a document should be.

Another problem associated with proxy caching occurs when a web page is cached on a remote network and that cached copy is then indexed by one or more of the search engine robots. The search sites have become the navigational hubs of the Internet; they are where nearly all users go to find what they're looking for. When web surfers use a search site that has indexed cached web pages, these digital clones can appear right next to, in front of or instead of the original, true sites.

As users follow a hyperlink to a cached page, chances are they will not find the information they're looking for. Most proxy-server software programmes deny access to cached web pages unless the request for information originates from within that particular network. Anyone outside the network will most likely be turned away. Three search sites have been identified that contain cached web pages. They are Excite, Infoseek and Alta Vista, some of the most popular and frequently visited sites on the Internet.

Cached documents are totally controlled by someone other than the original publisher. By altering the HTML of a cached web document and then passing the counterfeit version on as if it were the original – a process known as cache poisoning – an organisation's information such as e-mail address or requests for credit card information can be redirected elsewhere without the knowledge or consent of the original publisher.

When he was asked what was to stop tampering and cache poisoning, Vint Cerf, senior vice president of Internet Architecture and Engineering at MCI, said: 'Nothing other than judicious use of digital signatures, the effectiveness of which is strongly dependent on public key directories and the difficulty of forging a digital signature.' On the availability of strong encryption, in other words.

But according to Nathaniel Borenstein, chief scientist at First Virtual Holdings and current board member of Computer Professionals for Social Responsibility (CPSR): 'There is absolutely no technical remedy to this problem. Legal remedies might conceivably help if jurisdictional problems can be overcome. Some may claim that digital watermarking or other cryptographic authentication technologies are useful in this regard. The fact is that they can be very useful to an expert in proving such tampering after the event, but their proper use is sufficiently esoteric that it is basically the province of experts. I think it will always be easy to fool most Internet users into thinking they are looking at a valid page when they really aren't.'

Considering the opportunity for profit, the threat of cache abuse is significant enough to warrant attention to this issue. Based upon the premise that trust is a prerequisite for any financial payment system or network to be accepted, issues such as proxy caching must be addressed and resolved now; otherwise, the inadequacies of today's security technologies pose a significant risk to the future of electronic commerce on the Internet.

When Peter Neumann, principal scientist at SRI International and moderator of the RISKS Forum, was asked if these clearing houses of cached web pages will become primary targets for tampering, censorship, and abuse he replied: 'Absolutely yes. You might also expect that the FBI would want guaranteed surreptitious access to all caches – for example, for setting up stings and monitoring all accesses – much as they are seeking key-recovery mechanisms for crypto.'

According to Neumann: 'Any privacy-sensitive country would want to restrict the potential for data aggregation flowing outside its boundaries. Some countries would want to ensure that information relating to crime, kiddie porn, drugs, arms procurement, national security threats, etc., would not flow in. As is the case with all innovative technologies, there is a conflict between what is possible and what is sensible. The desire to lead a sound life in the presence of technology that is not secure, reliable, or safe is often at odds with the opportunities to take commercial advantage of weaknesses in the implementation of the technology and with desires of governments to control or monitor its citizens. There is also often a strong disconnect between national interests and international interests. The situation you are exploring is just one more instance.'

When asked about the effects of replication on censorship and privacy protection, Borenstein replied: 'This is one of the biggest threats. The most salient feature of this technology is that it makes it easier to try to censor the Internet. A small, repressive country could establish a choke point on its Internet traffic and effectively censor the entire Internet as seen from inside that country. Sophisticated users will be able to work around these restrictions, but governments may well be able to detect and prosecute such workarounds. Insofar as the caches are used even for access-controlled web pages, proxy caching and replication could have a very serious effect on privacy by exposing the access-controlled information to anyone who gets access to the cache.'

Borenstein summarised his views on proxy caching and the implementation of an international hierarchical cache system/global mesh by saying, 'It's a bad, bad idea.' As for suggesting possible alternatives: 'There aren't any problems proxy caching and replication solve that can't be solved by deploying more bandwidth. The answer is simple: more bandwidth. Provide more bandwidth, and the whole problem goes away.'

History has shown that privacy and security are not achieved through happenstance but by design. In the case of proxy caching, the apparent need on the part of network administrators for an immediate solution to the problem of congestion control should not take precedence over good judgment in responsible development of the Internet. We must consider the value and cost of designing and implementing network security mechanisms that take into account network performance expectations. As to the future development of the Internet, we must be willing to avoid shortsighted solutions and make the investments necessary to have the kind of communications network we shall want to use both tomorrow and in the years ahead. ❏

Russell Baird Tewksbury is a writer, researcher and consultant on Internet matters. This is an edited and updated version of an article originally published in the e-zine On The Internet

INDEX *presents an evening of* banned music

featuring
Simon Rattle *with*
Antony Pay, Robert Lloyd, Rex Lawson,
Philip Langridge, Tasmin Little, Lynn Harrell,
Jill Gomez, and Eleanora Bokova,

This is a unique opportunity to hear rarely performed banned pieces by:
Shostakovich, Messiaen, Poulenc,
Alan Bush and Conlon Nancarrow

At the Union Chapel, Islington
A beautiful Gothic building with a history of offering sanctuary to the dissenting voice
Monday 16 November,
for ticket information call Robin Oakley *on (44) 171 278 2313*

Index on Censorship relies on the generosity and support of our many friends and subscribers worldwide. We depend on donations to guarantee our independence and to support our projects which promote free expression.

Index on Censorship and *Writers and Scholars Educational Trust* would like to thank the following for their continued support:

Anonymous
The Ajahma Charitable Trust
The Arts Council of England
The Bromley Trust
Danish International Development Agency (DANIDA)
Demokratifonden
The European Commission
The Ford Foundation
Fritt Ord Foundation
The JM Kaplan Fund
The Goldberg Family Trust
The Lyndhurst Settlement
The Open Society Institute
Pearson plc Charitable Trust

The Prins Claus Fund
The Ruben and Elisabeth Rausing Trust
CA Rodewald Charitable Settlement
EJB Rose Charitable Trust
The Royal Literary Fund
The Royal Ministry of Foreign Affairs, Norway
The Alan and Babette Sainsbury Charitable Fund
Scottish Media Group plc
The Stephen Spender Memorial Fund
Tom Stoppard
Swedish International Development Co-operation Agency (Sida)
UNESCO
United News and Media plc

For details about the concert, or for other ways to support *Index on Censorship* contact:
Robin Oakley, Development Manager, on (44) 171 278 2313. Fax: 0171 278 1878
Index on Censorship, 33 Islington High Street, London N1 9HL